THE BOSTON MARATHON BOMBINGS, ONE YEAR ON: A LOOK BACK TO LOOK FORWARD

HEARING

BEFORE THE

COMMITTEE ON HOMELAND SECURITY
HOUSE OF REPRESENTATIVES

ONE HUNDRED THIRTEENTH CONGRESS

SECOND SESSION

APRIL 9, 2014

Serial No. 113–64

Printed for the use of the Committee on Homeland Security

Available via the World Wide Web: http://www.gpo.gov/fdsys/

U.S. GOVERNMENT PRINTING OFFICE

88–783 PDF   WASHINGTON : 2014

For sale by the Superintendent of Documents, U.S. Government Printing Office
Internet: bookstore.gpo.gov   Phone: toll free (866) 512–1800; DC area (202) 512–1800
Fax: (202) 512–2250   Mail: Stop SSOP, Washington, DC 20402–0001

COMMITTEE ON HOMELAND SECURITY

MICHAEL T. MCCAUL, Texas, *Chairman*

LAMAR SMITH, Texas
PETER T. KING, New York
MIKE ROGERS, Alabama
PAUL C. BROUN, Georgia
CANDICE S. MILLER, Michigan, *Vice Chair*
PATRICK MEEHAN, Pennsylvania
JEFF DUNCAN, South Carolina
TOM MARINO, Pennsylvania
JASON CHAFFETZ, Utah
STEVEN M. PALAZZO, Mississippi
LOU BARLETTA, Pennsylvania
RICHARD HUDSON, North Carolina
STEVE DAINES, Montana
SUSAN W. BROOKS, Indiana
SCOTT PERRY, Pennsylvania
MARK SANFORD, South Carolina
VACANCY

BENNIE G. THOMPSON, Mississippi
LORETTA SANCHEZ, California
SHEILA JACKSON LEE, Texas
YVETTE D. CLARKE, New York
BRIAN HIGGINS, New York
CEDRIC L. RICHMOND, Louisiana
WILLIAM R. KEATING, Massachusetts
RON BARBER, Arizona
DONDALD M. PAYNE, JR., New Jersey
BETO O'ROURKE, Texas
FILEMON VELA, Texas
ERIC SWALWELL, California
VACANCY
VACANCY

BRENDAN P. SHIELDS, *Staff Director*
MICHAEL GEFFROY, *Deputy Staff Director/Chief Counsel*
MICHAEL S. TWINCHEK, *Chief Clerk*
I. LANIER AVANT, *Minority Staff Director*

CONTENTS

THE BOSTON MARATHON BOMBINGS, ONE YEAR ON: A LOOK BACK TO LOOK FORWARD

Wednesday, April 9, 2014

U.S. HOUSE OF REPRESENTATIVES,
COMMITTEE ON HOMELAND SECURITY,
Washington, DC.

The committee met, pursuant to call, at 10:07 a.m., in Room 311, Cannon House Office Building, Hon. Michael T. McCaul [Chairman of the committee] presiding.

Present: Representatives McCaul, King, Broun, Meehan, Duncan, Chaffetz, Palazzo, Hudson, Brooks, Perry, Sanford, Sanchez, Clarke, Richmond, Keating, Payne, Vela, and Swalwell.

Chairman MCCAUL. The Committee on Homeland Security will come to order.

The committee is meeting today to continue a series of hearings examining the Boston bombings of April 15, 2013.

Today there will be a memorial service in my home State of Texas for the Fort Hood shooting that took place on April 2, 2014. So before we would continue this proceeding, I would like to take a moment of silence to recognize the victims of this horrific attack.

[Moment of silence.]

Chairman MCCAUL. I now recognize myself for an opening statement.

This is a powerful and emotional day for the witnesses and for me and this committee. It is a time to remember the anniversary of the Boston Marathon bombings, and it is a time to remember the victims.

I personally remember walking down Boylston Street with Boston Police Commissioner Ed Davis, who is with us here today. I remember him pointing out to me the trash cans where the bombs went off, injuring 260 innocent people and killing 3, including a little 8-year-old boy, in cold blood.

In the middle of the chaos, we also witnessed exceptional bravery. If not for the heroic acts of the first responders and Boston citizens who ran towards danger instead of away, many more could have died.

I remember after the attack the marathoners tying their shoes together in the hundreds in a memorial out of respect and out of dedication.

I also remember the Watertown police chief, who is with us here today as well—and thank you for being here—I remember him taking me and Congressman Keating on a tour of their once-quiet neighborhood and seeing the aftermath of the gunfight to take down two of the biggest terrorists since 9/11.

(1)

What happened after that is what heroes are made of. Tamerlan threw everything he had at these officers, including pipe bombs, rounds of ammunition, and a pressure-cooker IED. The Boston bomber was finally subdued after the heroic acts and efforts of our local law enforcement, who are with us today as well.

What is not so well-known is that, had it not been for the efforts of Commissioner Ed Davis and those of the Watertown police force, our Nation could have been further terrorized. These terrorists had six more bombs in their car, and they were on their way to Times Square. If it wasn't for these heroic acts of bravery, New York City could have been hit again.

We will hear from these brave individuals today for the first time before Congress.

This committee, through its oversight responsibilities, conducted a thorough investigation into what happened and what went wrong. We found that several flags and warnings were missed. We found that Tamerlan was on the radar of the FBI and somehow dropped off.

We found that Tamerlan traveled to Dagestan, known for its Chechen terrorists. This is precisely what the Russian letter warned our intelligence community and FBI about. He came back even more radicalized. We also found that, unfortunately, Customs, FBI, and the intelligence community somehow missed it. Arrogantly, some U.S. officials said it would not have made a difference—it would not have made a difference if they had known about his overseas travels.

We now know that a check of his public social media would have shown indicators, such as jihadist video postings. His mosque had seen escalating behavior, as well. It likely would have been clear that he was becoming more and more of a threat to the community.

Which takes me to my last point. State and local police have a strong role in counterterrorism. They know the streets better than anybody, and they know the local threats. The Boston PD should have been given more information throughout the entire process. They must know the terror threats in their own backyards—they know those. This process, in my judgment, has to change.

In an effort to do this, 2 weeks ago our committee issued our report about the Boston Marathon bombings. Over the course of the year, we held two hearings, had numerous briefings and engagements, traveled to Boston multiple times, had a bipartisan staff delegation travel to Moscow. I personally went to Boston and Moscow with Mr. Keating and spoke with officials on the ground.

I want to thank the Democrats for their participation in the investigation and the report, and I am pleased that their input was reflected in the final report.

Based on the lessons learned, we issued our findings and recommendations to fix some of the systemic problems that led to Tamerlan Tsarnaev falling off of our radar. I hope to think, in a small way, the recommendations we made in this report can make a difference in preventing the tragedy we saw in Boston from occurring again in the homeland.

I am pleased to know and to hear and report that both the FBI and DHS are already constructively implementing the recommendations of this committee's report, and I commend them for that. Let us hope that such a tragic event like this never happens again.

With that, I would now like to recognize the heroes in this hearing, in this committee room here today, the Watertown officers, who are with us here today, who were directly involved in Tamerlan's takedown and being taken off the streets once and for all: Sergeant Jeff Pugliese, Sergeant John MacLellan, Officer Joseph Reynolds, Officer Miguel Colon, Officer Michael Comick, and, of course, Chief Deveau.

Gentlemen, would you please stand and be recognized?

[Applause.]

[The statement of Chairman McCaul follows:]

STATEMENT OF CHAIRMAN MICHAEL T. MCCAUL

APRIL 9, 2014

This is a powerful and emotional day for the witnesses, for me, and this committee. It's a time to remember the anniversary of the Boston Marathon bombings, and it's a time to remember the victims. I, personally, remember walking down Boylston Street with Boston Police Commissioner Ed Davis, who is with us here today. I remember him pointing out to me the trash cans where the bombs went off, injuring 260 innocent people and killing 3 including a little 8-year-old boy, in cold blood.

In the middle of chaos, we also witnesses exceptional bravery. If not for the heroic acts of the first responders and Boston citizens who ran towards danger instead of away, many more could have died.

I remember after the attack, the marathoners tying their shoes together in the hundreds in a memorial out of respect and dedication. I remember the Watertown Police Chief, who is before us today. I remember him taking Congressman Keating and me on a tour of their once-quiet neighborhood and seeing the aftermath of the gunfight to take down two of the biggest terrorists since 9/11.

What happened after that is what heroes are made of. Tamerlan threw everything he had at these officers including pipe bombs, rounds of ammunition, and a pressure cooker IED. The Boston Bomber was finally subdued after the heroic acts and efforts of our local law enforcement, some of who are with us today.

What is not so well-known is that had it not been for the efforts of Commissioner Ed Davis and his efforts, and those of the Watertown police force, our Nation could have been further terrorized. These terrorists had six more bombs in their car and were on their way to Times Square. If it wasn't for these heroic acts of bravery New York City could have been hit again.

We will hear from these brave individuals today for the first time before Congress. This committee, through its oversight responsibilities, conducted a thorough investigation into what happened and what went wrong.

We found that several red flags and warnings were missed. We found that Tamerlan was on the radar of the FBI and somehow dropped off. We found that Tamerlan traveled to Dagestan, known for its Chechen terrorists. This is precisely what the Russian letter warned our intelligence community and FBI about. He came back even more radicalized. We also found that unfortunately Customs, FBI, and the IC somehow missed it. Arrogantly, some U.S. officials said "It would not have made a difference" if they had known about his overseas travel. We now know that a check of his public social media would have shown indicators such as Jihadists video postings. His Mosque had seen escalating behavior as well. It likely would have been clear that he was becoming more and more of a threat to the community.

Which takes me to me to my last point: State and local police have a strong role in counterterrorism. They know the streets better than anybody and they know the local threats. The Boston Police Department should have been given more information throughout the entire process. They must know the terror threats in their own backyards. This process in my judgment has to change.

In an effort to do this, 2 weeks ago our committee issued our report about the Boston Marathon bombings. Over the course of the year, we held two hearings; had numerous briefings and engagements; traveled to Boston multiple times; and had a bipartisan staff delegation travel to Moscow. I personally went to Boston and Moscow with Mr. Keating and spoke with officials on the ground. I want to thank the

Democrats for their participation in the investigation and the report, and I'm pleased that their input was reflected in the final report. Based on lessons learned, we issued our findings and recommendations to fix some of the systemic problems that led to Tamerlan Tsarnaev falling off of our radar.

I hope to think in a small way the recommendations we made in this report can make a difference in preventing the tragedy we saw in Boston from occurring again in the homeland. I am pleased to know, to hear, and to report that both the FBI and DHS are already constructively implementing the recommendations of this committee's report. Let us hope that such a tragic event like this never happens again.

Chairman MCCAUL. The Chairman now recognizes the acting Ranking Member, Ms. Sanchez.

Ms. SANCHEZ. I thank the Chairman for holding today's hearing.

I also extend my condolences to the families of the 4 people killed during last week's shooting at Fort Hood, and additional prayers are with the 16 people who were injured during that shooting. I do want to recognize the first-responder community and medical personnel for their incredible response to the shooting. As of today, the Joint Terrorism Task Force does not consider the shooting an act of terrorism. However, the investigation is still on-going.

I am going to read into the record the comments from our Ranking Member, Mr. Thompson of Mississippi, which I concur with.

Incidents like last week's shooting and last year's Boston Marathon bombing, the focus of today's hearing, remind us of the importance of our first responders. With that being said, I again commend the service of our witnesses—former Commissioner Davis, Chief Deveau, Sergeant Pugliese. I also thank Professor Leonard for recognizing their courageous efforts in his research.

Resilience and response are two of the reasons why almost a year ago the Boston metropolitan area—why almost a year from ago the Boston metropolitan area remains strong. I wish Mayor Walsh, president of the Boston Athletic Association Joann Flaminio, and all the runners and volunteers participating in the 118th Boston Marathon well as the race commences on the 21st of April of this year.

Even though Boston is standing strong, it would be a disservice to the community not to take a look back. There are still unanswered questions about the history of the Tsarnaev brothers, the alleged Boston Marathon bombers, and we owe it to the people of Boston and the rest of America to make sure that the appropriate officials do a thorough review of that situation.

Last April, the inspectors general of the intelligence community, Departments of Homeland Security and Justice, and the Central Intelligence Agency announced a joint investigation into whether intelligence was properly distributed and acted upon in the months and the years before the bombings at the Boston Marathon.

I find it rather unfortunate, however, that the review was delayed because of the senseless 16-day Government shutdown in October 2013. Partisan disagreements create serious gaps in homeland security oversight, and this is just one example of the myriad of setbacks that the shutdown yielded.

Another development since last year is Attorney General Holder's January 13 announcement that the United States would be seeking the death penalty against Tamerlan* Tsarnaev, the alleged Boston Marathon bomber. He was arrested and indicted, and I have de-

---

* See clarification, p. 33.

clared my confidence in his receiving a fair yet aggressive prosecution in the United States District Court for the Commonwealth of Massachusetts.

Mr. Chairman, as a former Federal prosecutor, you know Attorney General Holder's decision to seek the death penalty is a game-changer. I am sure you are familiar with the intricacies involved in a capital case.

As I reminded the committee last year, as we fulfill our Constitutional oversight responsibilities, we must be careful not to jeopardize a Federal prosecution. This applies in both the words that we speak to the public as well as the publications that stem from this committee.

Unfortunately, some of the actions that have extended from this committee have not been helpful to the Department of Justice. On March 26, a Majority staff report, endorsed by a minority of the Members of this committee, was released to the public. Less than 48 hours after the report's release, Tsarnaev's defense team filed a motion in the United States District Court citing this report.

I reemphasize that, as Members of Congress, especially as Members of the Homeland Security Committee, we are held to a heightened standard. We are trusted with both Classified and Unclassified briefings and meetings with the members of the intelligence community. Therefore, the words that we speak or we publish about alleged terrorists transcend the halls of this Congress and are not taken lightly by the public.

Furthermore, this not only applies to events surrounding Boston but also to other events with pending investigations. Reaching conclusions before facts are known puts the reputation of this committee at peril. Thus, we must exercise discretion in our questioning, in our statements about events, suspects, and the links to others that may not be in custody.

But in spite of those limitations, Mr. Chairman, we can still use our platform to have a productive discussion about the Boston Marathon bombing and act on outstanding matters. For example, we can and we should discuss the funding given to the first-responder community.

Last year, at the Committee on Homeland Security's first hearing on the Boston Marathon bombings, former Commissioner Davis stated that, without grant funding, "the response would have been much less comprehensive than it was." Without the exercises supported through the Urban Areas Security Initiative funding, there would be more people who died in these attacks.

Professor Leonard's testimony also indicates that this type of preparedness is what makes first response effective. Sargent Pugliese is also testifying today that local municipal governments are not financially equipped to take on the increasing burden of these catastrophic attacks like Boston.

It is time that we not only listen to the first responders but that we also take action.

Not only after last year's hearing but also hearings throughout several Congresses, Members have heard about the importance of these grant programs and the success stories involving them. Accordingly, I urge Members to oppose the administration's proposal to shift focus away from supporting State and local efforts to develop terrorism-related prevention and preparedness capabilities by morphing the Homeland Security Grant Program into an all-hazards grant.

I am not convinced that the administration's underfunded grant consolidation proposal would provide sufficient support for first responders across America to build and maintain the capabilities necessary to respond as effectively as the first responders in Boston and Watertown did after the bombings last year.

We learned from 9/11 that it is the local responders that are there on the scene. I cannot support any grant reform proposal until I am convinced that it would provide the support necessary to maintain the terrorism preparedness capabilities that we have spent building—building now for over a decade.

Also, I agree with the Chairman that we cannot ignore that information sharing between Federal, State, and local authorities needs strengthening. Since September 11, information-sharing silos that the 9/11 Commissioners recommended be addressed continue to be exposed after tragic events. We need to work together to develop ways to fix that problem as soon as possible.

We must also consider the economic cost of terrorism. In response to the events of September 11, Congress enacted the Terrorism Risk Insurance Act of 2002. That measure increased the availability of terrorism risk insurance to at-risk American businesses by guaranteeing that the Government would share some of the losses with private insurance should a terrorist attack occur at a building.

That act is set to sunset this year. According to the RAND Corporation, allowing this act to expire would harm our National security. Last year, Mr. Thompson introduced a bill that would extend the act and add some needed improvements, and I urge my colleagues to cosponsor that legislation.

Even though it has been almost a year since the bombings, there have been some game-changing moments, and some ships are still anchored. As we continue to seek answers, I remind us to be responsible and to act within our Constitutional boundaries. The people of Boston are looking for our leadership on this issue.

I yield back the balance of my time and ask that the full statement of Ranking Member Thompson be put into the record, Mr. Chairman.

Chairman MCCAUL. Without objection, so ordered. I thank the Ranking Member.

[The statement of Ranking Member Thompson follows:]

STATEMENT OF RANKING MEMBER BENNIE G. THOMPSON

APRIL 9, 2014

I want to extend condolences to the families of the 4 people killed during last week's shooting at Ft. Hood. Additionally, prayers are with the 16 people who were injured during the shooting. I want to recognize the first responder community and medical personnel for their incredible response to the shooting. As of today, the Joint Terrorism Task Force does not consider the shooting an act of terrorism. However, the investigation is still on-going.

Incidents like last week's shooting and last year's Boston Marathon bombing—the focus of today's hearing—remind us of the importance of first responders. With that being said, I again commend the service of our witnesses: Former Commissioner Davis, Chief Deveau, and Sergeant Pugliese. I also thank Professor Leonard for recognizing their courageous efforts in his research.

Resilience and response are two of the reasons why almost a year later the Boston metropolitan area remains strong. Hence, I wish Mayor Walsh, president of the Boston Athletic Association, Joann Flamino, and all the runners and volunteers participating in the 118th Boston Marathon well as the race commences on April 21.

Even though Boston is standing strong, it would be a disservice to the community not to take a look back. There are still unanswered questions about the history of Tsarnaev brothers—the alleged Boston Marathon bombers. We owe it to the people of Boston and the rest of America to make sure that the appropriate officials do a thorough review of the situation.

Last April, the inspectors general of the intelligence community, Departments of Homeland Security and Justice and the Central Intelligence Agency announced a joint investigation into whether intelligence was properly distributed and acted upon in the months and years before the bombings at the Boston Marathon. I find it rather unfortunate; however, that the review was delayed because of the senseless 16-day Government shut-down in October 2013. Partisan disagreements create serious gaps in homeland security oversight and this is just one example of the myriad of setbacks the shut-down yielded.

Another development since last year is Attorney General Holder's January 30 announcement that the United States would be seeking the death penalty against Dzhokar Tsarnaev, the alleged Boston Marathon bomber. Since Dzhokar Tsarnaev was arrested and indicted, I have declared my confidence in his receiving a fair, yet aggressive prosecution in the United States District Court for the Commonwealth of Massachusetts. Mr. Chairman, as a former Federal prosecutor, you know Attorney General Holder's decision to seek the death penalty against Tsarnaev was a game-changer. I am sure you are familiar with the intricacies involved in a capital case. As I reminded the committee last year, as we fulfill our Constitutional oversight responsibilities, we must be careful not to jeopardize a Federal prosecution—this applies to both the words we speak to the public as well as the publications that stem from our research.

Unfortunately, some of the actions that have extended from by this committee have not been helpful to the Department of Justice. On March 26, a Majority Staff Report endorsed by a minority of Members of this committee was released to the public. Less than 48 hours after the report's release, Dzohkar Tsarnaev's defense team filed a motion in the United States District Court citing this report. I reemphasize that as Members of Congress, especially Members of the Homeland Security Committee, we are held to a heightened standard. We are trusted to have both Classified and Unclassified briefings and meetings with the members of intelligence community.

Therefore, the words we speak or publish about an alleged terrorist transcend the halls of Congress and are not taken lightly by the public. Furthermore, this not only applies to events surrounding Boston but also to other events with pending investigation. Reaching conclusions before facts are known puts the reputation of this committee in peril. Thus, we must exercise discretion in our questioning and our statements about events, suspects, and the links to others that may not be in custody.

In spite of these limitations, Mr. Chairman, we can still use our platform to have a productive discussion about the Boston Marathon bombing and act on outstanding matters. For instance, we can and should discuss the funding given to the first-responder community.

Last year, at the Committee on Homeland Security's first hearing on the Boston Marathon bombings, former Commissioner Davis stated that without grant funding, the "response would have been much less comprehensive than it was" and without the exercises supported through Urban Area Security Initiative funding, "there would be more people who had died in these attacks." Professor Leonard's testimony also indicates that this type of preparedness is what made the first response effective. Sergeant Pugliese is also testifying today that local municipal governments are not financially equipped to take on the increasing burden of catastrophic attacks like Boston. It is time that we not only listen to the first responders but also take action.

Not only after last year's hearing, but also hearings throughout several Congresses, Members have heard about the importance of these grant programs and success stories involving them. Accordingly, I urge Members to oppose the administration's proposal to shift focus away from supporting State and local efforts to develop terrorism-related prevention and preparedness capabilities by morphing the Homeland Security Grant Program into an all hazards grant. I am not convinced that the administration's underfunded grant consolidation proposal would provide sufficient support for first responders across America to build and maintain the capabilities necessary to respond as effectively as the first responders in Boston and

Watertown did after the bombings last year. I cannot support any grant reform proposal until I am convinced that it would provide support necessary to maintain the terrorism-preparedness capabilities we have spent over a decade building.

Also, I agree with the Chairman that we cannot ignore that information sharing between Federal, State, and local authorities needs strengthening. Since September 11, information-sharing silos that the 9/11 Commissioners recommended be addressed continue to be exposed after tragic events. We need to work together to develop ways to fix this problem post-haste.

We must also consider the economic costs of terrorism. In response to the events of September 11, 2001, Congress enacted the Terrorism Risk Insurance Act of 2002. That measure increased the availability of terrorism risk insurance to at-risk American businesses by guaranteeing that the Government would share some of the losses with private insurers should a terrorist attack occur. That act is set to sunset this year. According to the RAND corporation, allowing this Act to expire would harm National security. Last year, I introduced a bill that would extend the Act and add some needed improvements. I urge my colleagues to cosponsor this legislation.

Even though it has been almost a year since the bombings, there have been some game-changing moments, and some ships are still anchored. As we continue to seek answers, I remind us to be responsible and act within our Constitutional boundaries. The people of Boston are looking for our leadership on this issue.

Chairman MCCAUL. As a former Federal prosecutor, I understand legal standards very well and would do nothing to jeopardize the prosecution.

I also, as a Member of Congress, understand our responsibilities and this committee's responsibilities of oversight under the Constitution of the United States. As recently quoted in the *Boston Globe,* "This shouldn't be about Democrats and Republicans. If you can't put that stuff behind you on an issue like this, then I don't know when you can." I couldn't agree more with the *Boston Globe* on that statement.

With that, the Chairman now recognizes the gentleman from Massachusetts, who has had more impact out of this tragedy than any other Member of this committee, Mr. Keating, to introduce today's witnesses.

Mr. KEATING. Thank you, Mr. Chairman.

By way of introduction, I just want to realize, have us all realize that it is almost a year to the day of April 15, when we were all shocked, not just in Massachusetts but around the country, at the news that the lives of four young individuals were taken and hundreds more were injured in the Boston Marathon.

If I could, in this introductory period, Mr. Chairman, I would like us to take a moment to remember and honor the lives of Krystle Campbell, 29; Sean Collier, 26; Lingzi Lu, 23; and Martin Richard, 8.

[Moment of silence.]

Mr. KEATING. There is no doubt that Boston's handling of the marathon attack will serve as a model for cities around the world on how to respond to mass homeland security incidents. For this reason, it is important to look back and analyze the steps taken before, during, and after the tragedy.

We are honored today to have before this committee public safety officials from Boston and Watertown whose actions directly impeded further damage and loss of lives during the attack and in the days following. In that regard, all of our witnesses today can provide unique perspective on the best methods to increase our Nation's resiliency, adaptability, and transparency within the homeland security realm.

Our first witness, former Boston Police Commissioner Edward Davis, is currently with the John F. Kennedy School of Government at Harvard University. Mr. Davis was appointed by another great leader during this period, former Boston Mayor Thomas Menino. In this role, Commissioner Davis led the Boston Police Department's response to the Boston Marathon bombing on April 15.

The heroic actions and quick thinking of the men and women under Mr. Davis' leadership, as well as that of the Massachusetts National Guard, Boston Fire Department, EMS services, medical personnel, and, indeed, civilians, led to the survival of 17 critically injured civilians.

I have known Mr. Davis throughout his 34 years of law enforcement. He served on the Lowell Police Department, was named superintendent to that police department in 1994. During this period, he was recognized for reducing the crime rate in Lowell quicker than any other superintendent in the United States of America in cities of over 100,000 residents.

Commissioner, thank you for your service and your service to the city of Boston, the Commonwealth, and to our country. It is an honor to have you with us here today, and we look forward to your testimony.

We also have joining the former commissioner the chief of police at the Watertown Police Department, Mr. Edward Deveau. Chief Deveau sits on the executive board of the Massachusetts Chiefs of Police Association and played a crucial role during the manhunt for Dzhokhar Tsarnaev. His leadership made National headlines when five of his officers found themselves in a battle that involved both gunfire and homemade explosives on a small street in Watertown.

Chief Deveau, it is my pleasure to see you again. We are all grateful for your service and for taking the time out of your busy marathon training to testify here today.

Finally, Sergeant Jeffrey Pugliese is the second generation of a Watertown police officer, and he also served in the U.S. Army. He was born and raised in Watertown.

Having been promoted to sergeant in 1993, he was on the night shift during the early hours of April 19, 2013, when he came to the assistance of his fellow officers on Laurel Street. After a grueling exchange of fire, he came within 6 feet of Tamerlan Tsarnaev and eventually chased the subject and tackled him to the ground, leaving him time to rush those hurt in the scene to the hospital.

Members of this committee had the opportunity to visit the scene and were able to see just amazing signs of heroism in the impressions that the bombs and bullets made throughout that street.

Sergeant, thank you for your incredible service.

Even though I am not introducing him, I want to thank Professor Dutch Leonard from Harvard University.

If I could, Mr. Chairman, for the record, ask unanimous consent that the report that Professor Leonard is going to talk about today be submitted in the record.

Chairman MCCAUL. Without objection, so ordered.*

Mr. KEATING. I yield back.

---

*The information has been retained in committee files.

Chairman MCCAUL. Professor Leonard, thank you for being here today, as well. The Kennedy School, I guess I am somewhat of an alumni, being in the fellows program. My best to the faculty and staff. I know you produced an excellent report and analysis of the Boston bombing, and I look forward to reading that and sharing my thoughts with you. Thanks so much for being here today.

Full written statements of the witnesses will appear in the record.

The Chairman now recognizes Commissioner Davis for 5 minutes for an opening statement.

STATEMENT OF EDWARD F. DAVIS III, FORMER COMMISSIONER, BOSTON POLICE DEPARTMENT, FELLOW, JOHN F. KENNEDY SCHOOL OF GOVERNMENT, HARVARD UNIVERSITY

Mr. DAVIS. Thank you, Mr. Chairman, Ranking Member Thomas, distinguished Members of the committee. Thank you for inviting me before you today to once again discuss the events of April 15, 2013, when the Boston Marathon and our Nation came under attack by a pair of extremist brothers.

Chairman MCCAUL. Commissioner, I don't believe your mike is on.

Mr. DAVIS. Sorry about that.

I came before you last May as commissioner of the Boston Police Department to offer my insights into the information sharing that occurred before and during the events of last April.

I also came to you on behalf of the Boston community and specifically four people whose voices could no longer be heard because of the attacks of these cowards. Once again, before I begin my remarks, I ask you to remember the lives of Martin Richard, Krystle Campbell, Lu Lingzi, and MIT Police Officer Sean Collier.

Let my comments today reflect that none of us should ever forget four lives that were senselessly cut too short by the events of that week.

Next Tuesday afternoon at 2:50 p.m. will mark the 1-year anniversary since two pressure-cooker bombs were detonated on Boylston Street, on a historic stretch of a Boston street that leads to one of the most inspirational sites an athlete can view: The finish line of the Boston Marathon.

A lot has changed in that 1 year. For the hundreds of victims wounded in the attacks, life has been altered. Yet, on a daily basis, we continue to see and hear the inspirational stories of those victims—stories like that of Adrianne Haslet-Davis of Boston, a professional dancer who returned to the stage last month despite losing part of her left leg in one of the explosions; or Jeff Bauman of Chelmsford. The iconic image of him being wheeled away from the devastation by a good Samaritan is emblazoned in our minds. He just announced he is engaged and is going to be a new father soon. Or Martin Richard's sister, Jane, whose recovery has inspired a team of runners to run on her behalf in this year's marathon. Or the dozens of nurses and first responders who will be undertaking their first marathon ever next week in honor of the victims whose lives they helped save.

There are literally hundreds more stories that I could share with you. I just want to make sure that none of them are lost to time as we continue to examine the events that led up to the attacks and the actions that unfolded in the days and weeks afterwards.

I also want to speak on behalf of a community, not just the Boston community or even simply metropolitan Boston, but the greater community at large. In the year since, as I have traveled across this country talking about the lessons learned from this tragedy, I have come to realize that the community that rallied behind the "Boston Strong" mantra numbers in the millions, because that is how aggrieved our Nation felt after these attacks on our freedom and the innocents caught in the path of these explosions.

In the weeks after last April's attack, many questions were raised about who knew what when and what kind of information was being shared between law enforcement agencies. I am here to tell you that throughout the past year the level of interagency cooperation and information sharing that has occurred between local, State, and Federal law enforcement agencies has been critical to ensuring that we found ourselves answers to the many questions that have been posed.

Within the first few minutes of hearing about the explosions on Boylston Street, my first phone call was to my friend and colleague, Rick DesLauriers, at the FBI. He and I worked side-by-side throughout the ensuing week, and I consider him a staunch friend and ally. He offered all of the services of the FBI and other agencies to make sure that we not only apprehended the terrorists responsible for the crime but also to ensure that our interagency collaboration affords all of our agencies the critical amount of information sharing needed for our organizations to operate at peak efficiency.

What all of us learned that week and in the ensuing 12 months, though, is just how big our community is beyond the partnerships within the levels of government. Our law enforcement community is obvious. With me today are some of my colleagues from the neighboring Watertown Police Department—and you will hear from those heroes in a minute—the community where the manhunt came to an end and a community that found its neighborhoods under siege like never before in our country's history.

Make no mistake about this: Boston Police, Watertown Police, none of our agencies could have enjoyed the success we achieved without the involvement of a much larger community, one that felt personally victimized by the attacks. That is the community which has come to be known as "Boston Strong."

In the past 12 months, "Boston Strong" has been used as a rallying cry for an indomitable spirit, a sign of resilience and perseverance. Our hometown baseball team, the Red Sox, showed its tenacity and found inspiration from its message to win a World Series. It came to personify our indefatigable patriotism and commitment to neighbor helping neighbor. In New England, we didn't just see "Boston Strong" as a cliched hashtag on Twitter; we see it as a proclamation that we stand together, united in the face of previously unimaginable atrocities and determined to hold fast to our ideals and basic tenets of freedom.

"Boston Strong" became an exclamation by a community that wants the world to know that it can rally in the face of adversity and, armed with the necessary information, can work with its government partners to achieve a safe and desired outcome to a horrible and senseless act of violence.

When he came to our city a few days after the attacks, President Obama told the world that Boston will run again, and he was right. We run to support the dreams and personal aspirations of every man and woman who will be lacing up their sneakers to complete the grueling course. We run for the ideals that this kind of event brings our community together to celebrate everything that is great about our city, our State, and our Nation. We run for the men and women and children who can't be there this year: Krystle Campbell, Lu Lingzi, Martin Richard, and Officer Sean Collier. All of us—Boston, Massachusetts; New England; the United States—we run together.

Thank you.

[The prepared statement of Mr. Davis follows:]

PREPARED STATEMENT OF EDWARD F. DAVIS, III

APRIL 9, 2014

Chairman McCaul, Ranking Member Thompson, distinguished Members of the committee, thank you for inviting me back before you today to once again discuss the events of April 15, 2013, when the Boston Marathon and our Nation came under attack by a pair of extremist brothers bent on challenging our freedom.

I came before you last May as commissioner of the Boston Police Department to offer my insights into the information sharing that occurred before and during the events of last April. I also came to you on behalf of the Boston community, and specifically, four people whose voices could no longer be heard because of the attacks of these cowards.

Once again, before I begin my remarks, I ask that you remember the lives of Martin Richard, Krystle Campbell, Lu Lingzi, and MIT Police Officer Sean Collier. Let my comments today reflect that none of us should ever forget four lives that were senselessly cut too short by the events of that week.

Next Tuesday afternoon at 2:50 p.m. we will mark the 1-year anniversary since two pressure-cooker bombs were detonated on Boylston Street, on a historic stretch of a Boston Street that leads to one of the most inspirational sights an athlete can view—the finish line of the Boston Marathon.

A lot has changed in that 1 year. For the hundreds of victims wounded in the attacks, life has been altered. Yet on a daily basis, we continue to see and hear the inspirational stories of those victims—stories like that of Adrianne Haslet-Davis of Boston, a professional dancer who returned to the stage last month despite losing part of her left leg in one of the explosions. Or Jeff Bauman of Chelmsford—the iconic image of him being wheeled away from the devastation by a Good Samaritan is emblazoned in our minds. He just announced he's engaged and is going to be a new father soon. Or Martin Richard's sister Jane, whose recovery has inspired a team of runners to run on her behalf in this year's marathon. Or the dozens of nurses and first responders who will be undertaking their first marathon ever next week, in honor of the victims whose lives they helped save. There are literally hundreds more stories that I could share with you. I just want to make sure none of them are lost to time, as we continue to examine the events that led up to the attacks and the actions that unfolded in the days and weeks afterwards.

I also want to speak on behalf of a community. Not just a Boston community, or even simply Metropolitan Boston, but the greater community at large. In the year since, as I have travelled across this country talking about the lessons learned from this tragedy, I have come to realize the community that rallied behind the Boston Strong mantra numbers in the millions, because that is how aggrieved our Nation felt after these attacks on our freedoms and the innocents caught in the path of those explosions.

In the weeks after last April's attack, many questions were raised about who knew what when, and what kind of information was being shared between law enforcement agencies.

I am here to tell you that throughout this past year, the level of inter-agency co-operation and information sharing that has occurred between local, State, and Federal law enforcement agencies has been critical to ensuring that we have found answers to as many questions as we could pose.

Within the first few minutes of hearing about the explosions on Boylston Street, my first phone call was to my friend and colleague Rick Deslauriers at the FBI. He and I worked side-by-side throughout the ensuing week, and I consider him a staunch friend and ally. He offered all of the services of the FBI and other agencies to make sure that we not only apprehended the terrorists responsible for this crime, but also to ensure that our inter-agency collaboration affords all of our agencies the critical amount of information sharing needed for our organizations to operate at peak efficiency.

What all of us learned that week and in the ensuing 12 months, though, is just how big our community is beyond the partnerships within the levels of government. Our law enforcement community is obvious. With me today are some of my colleagues from the neighboring Watertown Police Department, the community where the manhunt came to an end and a community that found its neighborhoods under siege like never before in our country's history.

Make no mistake about this—Boston Police, Watertown police—none of our agencies could have enjoyed the successes we achieved without the involvement of a much larger community, one that felt personally victimized by the attacks. That is the community which has come to be known as Boston Strong.

In the past 12 months, Boston Strong has been used a rallying cry for an indomitable spirit, a sign of resilience and perseverance. Our hometown baseball team, the Red Sox, showed its tenacity and found inspiration from its message to win a World Series. It came to personify our indefatigable patriotism and commitment to neighbor helping neighbor. In New England, we don't just see Boston Strong as a clichéd hashtag on twitter, as see it as a proclamation that we stand together, united in the face of previously-unimaginable atrocity, and determined to hold fast to our ideals and basic tenets of freedom. Boston Strong became an exclamation by a community that wants the world to know that it can rally in the face of adversity and, armed with the necessary information, can work with its governmental partners to achieve a safe and desired outcome to a horrible and senseless act of violence.

Anyone who has ever visited Boston in the spring, or spent any time there, you know that the Boston Marathon is the People's Race. This is a 26.2-mile line that starts in Hopkinton, winds through Ashland, Framingham, Natick, Wellesley, Newton, and Brookline before ending in the heart of downtown Boston. And it occurs, appropriately enough, on Patriots' Day, a State holiday in Massachusetts that helps recognize the birth of the American Revolution, but has also come to embody our patriotic love for our community and our country. In New England, you either watch the marathon, you know somebody who runs it, or you run in it yourself. I had close friends and colleagues running in last year's race, many of whom were pressed into immediate service by the explosions. The marathon is part of our fiber, and an attack on the institution is an attack on our community as a whole.

This is the same community who waited anxiously as the largest manhunt in New England history played out over 4 days. When law enforcement decided to release the photos of the two suspects, we knew the dissemination of information into the hands of the public would be one of the most effective ways we could apprehend the individuals we wanted.

As we saw it play out on Thursday and Friday of that week, when the suspects took to the run, and began endangering innocents in other communities, we had to take the unprecedented action of asking more than half a million people to shelter in place while we search for these two men, who were throwing bombs at the police officers trying to catch them.

And for that historic Friday after the marathon, when we asked our communities to work with us and remain at home to keep the streets clear so we could do our job, they listened.

They listened because they shared a common goal, of wanting us to catch the men responsible. They listened because they trusted law enforcement, and by extension, their Government, to take care of them.

As anyone who has followed my career with the Boston and Lowell Police Departments knows, I believe in community policing, and the critical role that our residents play in helping to keep a community safe. It was relationships built before the marathon attacks that allowed us to implement such drastic measures, and those relationships only grew stronger when our communities saw the professional responses from their police agencies.

Sir Robert Peel was the Conservative Prime Minister of the United Kingdom in the early 1800s, and helped establish some of the modern concepts of our Nation's police forces.

It was Peel who said "The police are the public and the public are the police—the police being only members of the public who are paid to give full-time attention duties which are incumbent on every citizen in the interests of community welfare and existence."

Nearly 2 centuries later, that basic tenet still holds true today.

Together, we solve problems.

In the case of the multi-agency responses required in the wake of the attacks, yes, we did identify some areas we could improve upon, especially in terms of information sharing. But I remain supremely proud of the work done not just by the first officers, firefighters, or EMS workers who responded to the attacks, but also by the sea of yellow-jacketed Boston Marathon volunteers, and the runners who stopped short of their 26.2-mile goal to help innocent people suffering on the sidewalks along Boylston Street.

Beyond the successes we have achieved with the cooperation of the media agencies that cover our agencies, we also learned quickly what a valuable information tool our social media networks could be to us as that week unfolded last April. Systems that remain in place a year later, and allow our agencies to more effectively and more rapidly communication directly with the men and women we are sworn to serve and protect.

Next Monday, an historic number of runners will take to the pavement again to run in the fabled Boston Marathon, and next Monday, they will be protected by an historic amount of law enforcement personnel from among a wide swath of agencies, all of whom have been meeting on a regular basis for months to ensure the safety of everyone who will be running and watching the event. We are all working together.

When he came to our city a few days after the attacks, President Obama told the world that Boston will run again, and he was right.

We run to support the dreams and personal aspirations of every man and woman who will be lacing up their sneakers to complete the grueling course.

We run for the ideals that this kind of event brings our community together to celebrate everything that is great about our city, our State, and our Nation.

And we run for the men, women, and children who can't be there this year—Krystle Campbell, Lu Lingzi, Martin Richard, and Officer Sean Collier.

All of us—Boston, Massachusetts, New England, the United States—we run together.

Chairman MCCAUL. Thank you, Commissioner.

The Chairman now recognizes Chief Deveau for an opening statement.

STATEMENT OF EDWARD P. DEVEAU, CHIEF OF POLICE, WATERTOWN POLICE DEPARTMENT

Chief DEVEAU. Chairman McCaul, it is an honor to come before you and your committee. Thank you for the privilege of doing that.

I am extremely proud to be here today representing the men and women of the Watertown Police Department. Our goal has always been to be the best police department in Massachusetts.

Mr. Chairman, I had the privilege of meeting you and other Members of your distinguished committee when you traveled to Boston and Watertown. I want to thank you and your Members who took the time to learn about how the Watertown Police Department and the Watertown community responded to the events of that day.

Before I speak about the actions of the Watertown Police Department, I would like to give you some background on the events of last year.

Patriots' Day is a special day in Boston. It is my favorite weekend of the year. Businesses and schools are closed in Massachusetts for most people. Spectators line the 26 miles of the Boston

Marathon route from Hopkinton to Boston, cheering on the elite runners but also the regular people who run—many of them run for charities. The Boston Red Sox play at 11:00 a.m., and, after the game, all the fans walk down to Kenmore Square and watch the final mile or 2 of the marathon.

You haven't lived in Boston very long if you haven't been a spectator, a volunteer, or a runner. This year, I will run with 12 of my officers. It is going to be an emotional day for my officers as we run that route and cross the finish line on Boylston Street.

The Boston Marathon will be held in less than 2 weeks, and more people than ever want to be part of it. They want to come together to celebrate and remember those who died and those who were injured in last year's explosions. They want to remember Officer Sean Collier of the MIT Police Department, who was ambushed and killed before the two brothers headed to Watertown.

We have all seen what occurred at the finish line of the marathon on April 19, and Commissioner Davis has spoken about that and how well and impressive his department responded that day.

I am here today to talk about the events that occurred in Watertown in the early morning hours of April 19. That seemingly quiet overnight shift suddenly turned into a war zone. For the first time in America, police officers were attacked with guns and bombs, and it happened on a quiet backstreet of my community. Those two brothers were trying kill my police officers and had plans to kill and injure more innocent people.

The handful of Watertown officers on duty that night acted heroically and defended Watertown without regard for their own personal safety. They displayed courage and bravery as they stubbornly defended our community. Just as in Boston, my officers were at their very best when confronted with the biggest challenge of their careers. Their split-second decisions and actions went far beyond their academy training, but I can assure you, Mr. Chairman, it will now be taught in academies across the country.

It has been said before but, as their police chief, I want to state it again: The actions of my officers saved lives here in Boston and in New York City.

I want to introduce those officers, and you have already done that, Mr. Chairman, but, again, I would like to point out Officer Joe Reynolds, who was the first officer to confront those two brothers. Had no idea who he was up against. When we got notified in Watertown, we didn't know it was related to the Boston bombings, we didn't know it was related to Sean Collier. Joe stopped that car and was immediately shot on.

John MacLellan, who is sitting behind him, was the next officer there to come onto that street. Got a round right through his windshield, glass in his face, and the bullet went right by his ear. And those two guys continued to fight on that backstreet of Watertown.

Miguel Colon and Mike Comick showed up shortly after that. When Officer Colon showed up, he tried to put a spotlight down the street, and it was immediately shot out. He had trouble even getting out of his cruiser to help.

You are going to hear from Sergeant Pugliese and all the heroic things he did.

Mr. Chairman, during these trying days last April, two individuals attempted to strike fear and take down a city. They attempted to terrorize us all. In the end, they accomplished nothing. They will never know what it is—when America gets knocked down, we pick ourselves up and become even stronger. We will not be intimidated.

Watertown is stronger, Boston is stronger, and, in my opinion, the entire country is united and stronger. The strength and resilience and even defiance is what made Boston strong. I know if an attack occurs in another city within our country, they will respond in a similar way.

The Watertown police officers on duty that night stopped these evil brothers from leaving with a carful of weapons to carry out their deadly plan. In the following 18 hours, our entire department of 65 officers was tested and worked around the clock to keep our community safe. We received unprecedented support from surrounding police departments and Federal agencies. As a result, the second Boston bombing suspect was finally captured.

I want to thank the residents of Watertown for their patience and cooperation that day and for their continued support. It truly took an entire community.

Mr. Chairman, when I began my comments today, I mentioned our goal was to be the best police department in the State, and I am not sure if we have reached that, but I can tell you one thing. For 8½ minutes, we were the best damn police department in the world.

Mr. Chairman, I conclude my remarks, and I am happy to answer any questions you and your committee may have. Thank you.

[The prepared statement of Chief Deveau follows:]

PREPARED STATEMENT OF EDWARD P. DEVEAU

Chairman McCaul it is an honor to come before the U.S. House of Representatives Committee on Homeland Security.

I am extremely proud to be here today representing the men and women of the Watertown, Massachusetts Police Department. Our goal has always been to be the best police department in the State of Massachusetts.

Mr. Chairman, I had the privilege of meeting you and the other Members of your distinguished committee when you traveled to Boston and Watertown. I want to thank you and your Members who took the time to learn more about how the Watertown Police Department and the Watertown community responded to the events of last April.

Before I speak about the actions of the Watertown Police Department I would like to give you some background on the events of last year:

Patriot's Day is a special day in Boston and my favorite weekend of the year. Businesses and schools are closed in Massachusetts so most people have the day off. Spectators line the 26 miles of the Boston Marathon from Hopkinton to Boston cheering on elite runners from all around the world, and the regular people, including so many that run for charities.

The Boston Red Sox play at 11:00 a.m. and after the game all the fans walk down to Kenmore Square to watch the final mile or 2 of the marathon. You haven't lived in Boston very long if you haven't been a spectator, volunteer, or a runner. This year I will run with 12 of my officers, it will be an emotional moment when we cross the finish line on Boylston Street.

The Boston Marathon will be held in less than 2 weeks, and more people than ever want to be a part of it. They want to come together to celebrate and remember those who died and those who were injured in last year's explosions. They want to remember Officer Sean Collier of the MIT Police Department who was ambushed and killed before the two brothers headed to Watertown.

We have all seen what occurred at the finish line of the Boston Marathon on April 15 and Commissioner Ed Davis will speak about those tragic events and the Boston Police Department's impressive response that day.

I am here today to talk about the events that occurred in Watertown in the early morning hours of April 19. That seemingly quiet overnight shift suddenly turned into a war zone. For the first time in America, police officers were attacked with guns and bombs and it happened on a quiet backstreet in my community. Those two brothers were trying to kill my police officers and had plans to kill and injure more innocent people.

The handful of Watertown officers on duty that night acted heroically and defended Watertown without regard for their own personal safety. They displayed courage and bravery as they stubbornly defended our community. Just as in Boston, my officers were at their very best when confronted with the biggest challenge of their careers. Their split-second decisions and actions went far beyond their police academy training, but I can ensure you it will now be taught in police academies across the country. It has been said before Mr. Chairman, but as their police chief I want to state it again, the actions my officers took saved many more people from being killed and injured.

I want to introduce the officers that have accompanied Sgt. Pugliese and myself here today. Each of these officers played a key role in that historic gun battle on Laurel Street.

Mr. Chairman, during those trying day's last April two individuals attempted to strike fear and take down a city. They attempted to terrorize us all. In the end they accomplished nothing. What they will never know is that when America gets knocked down we pick ourselves up and become even stronger. We will not be intimidated. Watertown is stronger, Boston is stronger, and in my opinion the entire country is more united and stronger. The strength, resilience, and defiance is what made Boston Strong and I know if an attack occurs in any city within our country they will respond in a similar way.

The Watertown police officers on duty that night stopped these terrorists from leaving with their car full of weapons to carry out their next deadly plan. In the following 18 hours our entire department of 65 officers was tested and worked around the clock to keep our community safe. We received unprecedented support from surrounding police departments and Federal agencies. As a result the second Boston Marathon bombing suspect was finally captured.

I want to thank the residents of Watertown for their patience and cooperation that day and for their continuing support. It truly took an entire community.

Mr. Chairman, when I began my comments today I mentioned our goal was to be the best police department in our State and I am not sure if we have accomplished that, but what I do know is that for 8½ minutes on a back street in Watertown we were the best police department in the world.

Mr. Chairman, I conclude my remarks and I am happy to try and answer any questions your committee may have. Thank you.

Chairman MCCAUL. Thank you, Chief, for that compelling testimony. You are right, for 8½ minutes you were the best police department in the world.

With that, the Chairman now recognizes Sergeant Pugliese for his testimony.

STATEMENT OF JEFFREY J. PUGLIESE, SERGEANT, WATERTOWN POLICE DEPARTMENT

Sergeant PUGLIESE. Good morning. Thank you for inviting me to speak here this morning.

A little background on myself. I have been a police officer for 34 years in the Watertown Police Department.

Chairman MCCAUL. Is the mike on? Can the clerks help with the microphones at the witness table?

Sergeant PUGLIESE. Is that better?

Background on myself. Been a police officer for 34 years in the town of Watertown. Prior to that, I served in the U.S. Army from 1974 through 1978 in the military police assigned to Berlin, Germany, in the Berlin Brigade.

What happened that night is, it was just after midnight. I had finished my work shift when I heard a radio broadcast that officers from my agency were following an alleged carjacked vehicle. I knew that the current shift had four patrol officers and a patrol supervisor on the street that night, and so I thought I would head up to assist the officers in the event that it became a pursuit or a foot pursuit or any assistance was needed.

While en route to the area, I heard another broadcast that the officers were now taking gunfire from the occupants of the alleged carjacked vehicle and they were requesting assistance.

When I arrived on the scene, I heard gunfire. I exited my vehicle, and within moments I heard an explosion. I advanced to the area where the other officers were taking cover and returning gunfire.

The suspects were eventually taken into custody. I am not really at liberty to go into minute detail into the incident, as one of the suspects is still awaiting trial, but I will endeavor to answer any questions you may have.

I would like to make note that, in today's ever-changing environment of violence, local and municipal governments are not financially equipped to take on the increasing burden of such hostile actions.

In closing, I would like to say that all of the officers in the Watertown Police Department, those officers that were there that night, they are ordinary guys who were put in an extraordinary situation and performed extraordinarily well.

Once again, thank you for inviting me to speak at this hearing.

[The prepared statement of Sergeant Pugliese follows:]

PREPARED STATEMENT OF JEFFREY J. PUGLIESE

APRIL 9, 2014

Good morning, thank you for inviting me to speak here this morning. My name is Jeffrey J. Pugliese, I'm a police sergeant with the Watertown Massachusetts Police Department. I'm a 34-year veteran of the Department. In addition to my duties as a patrol supervisor, I have been a department firearms instructor for over 29 years. I am also a U.S. Army Veteran (1974–1978), serving in the Berlin, Germany as a military police officer assigned to the Berlin Brigade.

I am here to discuss the events of the early morning hours of April 19, 2013.

It was just after midnight and I had just finished my work shift when I heard a radio broadcast that officers from my agency were following an alleged carjacked vehicle. I knew the current shift had only four patrol officers and a patrol sergeant working, I decided to drive in that direction in the event any additional assistance would be needed by the officers.

While en route to the area, I heard another radio broadcast that officers were now taking gun fire from the occupants of the alleged carjacked vehicle and they were requesting assistance.

On arrival at the scene, I heard gun fire, I exited my vehicle and within moments I heard an explosion.

I advanced to the area where other officers were taking cover and returning gunfire. The suspects were eventually taken into custody.

While I am not at liberty to go into minute details as the incident is still awaiting trial of one of the suspects, I will endeavor to answer any questions you may have.

I think it should be noted that in today's ever-changing environment of violence, local municipal governments are not financially equipped to take on the increasing burden of such hostile actions.

In closing, I would like to say that all of the officers involved in this incident are ordinary men who were put into an extraordinary situation and performed extraordinarily well.

Once again, thank you for inviting me to speak here this morning.

Chairman MCCAUL. Thank you, Sergeant. Thanks for your act of heroism, taking down the biggest terrorists since 9/11. We appreciate what you did.

The Chairman now recognizes Professor Leonard for 5 minutes.

STATEMENT OF HERMAN "DUTCH" B. LEONARD, PROFESSOR OF PUBLIC MANAGEMENT, JOHN F. KENNEDY SCHOOL OF GOVERNMENT, HARVARD UNIVERSITY

Mr. LEONARD. Thank you, Mr. Chairman.

I want to thank Chairman McCaul and Ranking Member Thompson for inviting me to testify. My thanks also to Congressman Keating for his tireless work that has brought so much of the Boston Marathon set of issues to our attention.

I am honored to appear today with three of the genuine heroes of that week—Commissioner Ed Davis and Chief Ed Deveau and Sergeant Pugliese—and also to be together with all five of the Watertown police officers, who gave such a great account of themselves in that gun battle in those 8 minutes when they were the best police force in the world. Each of them will tell you that he is not a hero, but I feel very strongly today and I think we all know that we are in the company of heroes.

I am Dutch Leonard, the professor and co-director of the Program on Crisis Leadership at the Kennedy School of Government at Harvard. For the last year, Arnold Howitt, Christine Cole, Phil Heymann, and I have been doing research on the Boston Marathon bombing, supported in part by the International Centre for Sport Security.

This was a team effort from the beginning, and all of my colleagues were huge contributors to this. One of my co-authors, Christine Cole, is here with us today. The views I am presenting here are our own, not those of Harvard University or any other organization.

Our work was presented in honor and in memory of those who lost their lives or suffered grievous injuries in the Boston Marathon bombing, and it is dedicated to all of those who helped.

We focused on the issues of command and coordination. Others on our team are examining issues, as the committee has, of pre-event intelligence. Our report, entitled "Why was Boston Strong?", was released last week. The title refers to the local description, already referenced here, "Boston Strong," of the resilience shown by first responders and by survivors and by the wider community during that week.

My first message to the committee is about the first-responder part of "Boston Strong." Incident command works. The National Incident Management System that this committee mandated in the Homeland Security Act of 2002, Section 502, Part 5, is starting to work.

Before NIMS, first responders worked without an effective multi-agency doctrine of how to combine in incident management. Too many times, we watched while vitally-needed capabilities were not effectively deployed but instead were idled by a lack of ability to coordinate and execute across agencies, jurisdictional boundaries, and levels of government. NIMS is now starting to work, and "Boston Strong" is a good illustration of what can be achieved. We believe that the response in Boston over the course of that week was as good as one could reasonably have hoped.

So why were people and organizations able to be so effective? We found three answers.

First, because senior commanders, including Ed Davis and Ed Deveau, were able to come rapidly together to form an effective joint command and coordination structure.

Second, that was not due to chance. It resulted from thousands of hours of joint planning, exercises, and operations, combining numerous agencies over many years in the planning for and production of fixed events, some of it funded through grants from the Homeland Security Department.

Third, other communities can do this too. Any community can engage in joint planning and execution for any major fixed event. Paying your dues on good days builds the infrastructure of interagency familiarity, respect, and trust and has an immediate payoff. If a bad day ever comes, as it did in Boston, that infrastructure is literally a life-saver.

Our research also suggested several areas where further work needs to be done, but if we had to choose just one thing to improve, it would be to add at the tactical level an effective doctrine for what we call micro-command, the ability of people quickly to come together in an organized way. That would be in parallel to the National Incident Management System doctrine of macro-command, which allows the senior people to come together at the strategic level.

My second message today to the committee is about the community part of resistance to terrorism, which is again on display this year as my daughter and Chief Deveau and thousands of others train to run in this year's marathon.

"Boston Strong" encompasses what everyone did and does to stand tall and proud in the face of two murderous thugs with terrorist intent. "Boston Strong" is not a form of hubris or arrogance or naivete. It is a form of pride and defiance and resilience.

Terrorists, in the end, are few and weak. They could never defeat us, but we could voluntarily surrender to them, and we must not. If we cower in fear, if we abandon our commitment to a free and open society, then we do their work for them. We cannot defend the American way of life, as these five officers did that night, by surrendering it.

Preserve, protect, uphold, and defend. "Boston Strong" affirms the oath of office. "Boston Strong" says that we will defend the American way of life by continuing to participate in it. The community part of "Boston Strong" is a pretty good place to start in thinking about what resilience actually looks like.

Thank you, and I look forward to your questions.

[The prepared statement of Mr. Leonard follows:]

PREPARED STATEMENT OF HERMAN B. "DUTCH" LEONARD

APRIL 9, 2014

I would like to thank Chairman McCaul and Ranking Member Thompson for inviting me to testify today, as well as Congressman Keating of Massachusetts for the tireless work he has done to advance understanding of the events surrounding the Boston Marathon bombing that took place during the week of April 15, 2013.

I would also like to say that it is an honor for me to appear on this panel today with three of the genuine heroes of that week—Commissioner Ed Davis, Chief Ed Deveau, and Sgt. Jeff Pugliesi. One of the privileges of doing the research we have been carrying out is that we have regularly been in the presence of heroes—as I am again, and indeed as we all are today.

My name is Herman Leonard, known to my friends as "Dutch." I am the Baker Professor of Public Management at the Kennedy School of Government at Harvard University, where I am also faculty co-director of the Program on Crisis Leadership. I am also the Snider Family Professor of Business Administration and faculty co-chair of the Social Enterprise Initiative at Harvard Business School.

Over the course of the last year, since the bombs exploded at the finish line of the Boston Marathon, I have been working together with Arnold Howitt, who is executive director of the Ash Center for Democratic Governance and faculty co-director of the Program on Crisis Leadership, and Christine Cole, who is executive director of Harvard's Program on Criminal Justice Policy and Management, both at the Kennedy School, and with Professor Phillip Heymann of Harvard Law School to understand the sources of the strengths and weaknesses of the response to the marathon bombing. Our work was supported in part by the International Centre for Sport Security. In providing this testimony today, I am appearing as a representative of our research team; the views I am presenting here are our own, and not those of Harvard University or any other organization. This was a team effort, and while I'm providing the testimony today this work is the product of many hands. (Any errors made here, however, are mine.)

Our work was presented in honor and memory of those who lost their lives or suffered grievous injuries in the Boston Marathon bombing. It is dedicated to all of those who helped.

Our work focused on the issues of command within and coordination among the agencies and organizations involved in the response. Events like the Marathon bombing create a surge of demands and thereby create the need for sudden teams—groups of individuals and organizations, thrown together by circumstance even though they may not have worked together before, who must, in order to produce the best possible overall response, work effectively in tandem under conditions of uncertainty and stress in a rapidly-evolving situation. Our work concerns the response that began when the bombs exploded. Since we are seeking to understand and explain the quality of that response, we also focus on the extensive efforts made in advance to create the conditions that enabled it. Another part of our research team is examining some of the issues about pre-event intelligence; that work is not yet complete, and lies beyond the scope of the report I'm describing today.

We conducted a series of extended interviews, mainly with senior command officials in the major organizations involved in the response to the bombing. We also drew extensively on public statements and media descriptions of the events. Three weeks ago, we convened an "expert dialogue," gathering about 100 people, including many of the principals we had interviewed and other participants in the events of that terrible week, together with senior emergency management officials and academics from around the United States and from abroad. We spent an intensive day discussing the events and our proposed recommendations.

Our report, entitled "WHY was Boston Strong?," was released last week. Our title references the local description—"Boston Strong"—of the full spectrum phenomenon of response and resistance and resilience shown by first responders and by survivors and by the wider community during that week and since.

I appreciate this opportunity to discuss some of the findings of our research with you.

I have two simple messages for you today.

The first message is about the first responder part of Boston Strong that was on display last April.

That message is this: It works! Incident command works! When you build it in advance and use it in the moment, incident command is effective. The National Incident Management System is starting to work.

It has been a long time in coming and it is long overdue—but we've made a lot of progress Nationally, and the events in Boston last year put that vividly on display.

For something like 50 years, starting in the 1960s and continuing with greater energy after a devastating fire in California in 1970, people of goodwill in emergency management sought to develop and promulgate an effective, unified, coherent doctrine of incident management so that agencies and organizations that find themselves having to work together on terrible and dark days can efficiently and smoothly combine their capabilities and resources. The central purpose of having a single, unified approach is to enable a sudden team to produce the best performance reasonably possible given the nature of the challenge and the capacities that they have available. Too many times we have watched while vitally needed and clearly existing capabilities were not marshaled or effectively deployed—but instead were idled by a lack of ability to organize, coordinate, and execute across agencies, jurisdictional boundaries, and levels of government.

Finally, Congress—through the House Select Committee on Homeland Security, the original inception of this committee, in Part 5 of Section 502 of Public Law 107–296, the Homeland Security Act of 2002—mandated that the Secretary of Homeland Security build "a comprehensive national incident management system with Federal, State, and local government personnel, agencies, and authorities, to respond to . . . attacks and disasters." In 2004, the Department of Homeland Security duly issued instructions to those it could command directly (and created incentives for those it could not) to organize themselves for emergency response purposes in compliance with the structures and precepts and procedures of that system. FEMA has since worked to develop the system further and to help Federal and other agencies implement the structures, procedures, and training associated with making this doctrine a practical reality.

This mandate did not immediately succeed in enhancing performance in multiagency response to crisis events. In 2006, I gave testimony before the Senate Homeland Security Committee about Hurricane Katrina; incident management in the crucial early days of that response had been only sporadically applied and while it had proved helpful in the areas where it was used effectively it was clear that we were still a long way from having a fully operational National Incident Management System that worked smoothly across agencies of all types and all levels of government and all jurisdictions.

My first message to you today is that it is now working far better. Boston Strong is a good illustration of what can be—and, in Boston and in other communities where significant efforts have been made, has been—achieved. There is more to do, as I will suggest—but the first and most important thing to note is that for those communities that make the effort, creating an integrated incident command process that will work in the moment is a goal that is demonstratedly within reach.

There were some quite remarkably effective elements of the response in the aftermath of the bombing in Boston. As an example, the bombs caused literally dozens of fatal injuries, but, mercifully, there were only three fatalities on that terrible day. All of the seriously injured people were removed from the scene within 22 minutes. Every person who left the scene alive is alive today. The scene was rapidly secured and swept for additional explosive devices. It was then secured as a crime scene, collaboratively, using FBI and local and State assets, and the investigation was launched. Video from private and public surveillance cameras was quickly collected, additional photographic evidence (mainly from media and bystanders who volunteered their photographs and videos) was obtained, and an exhausting search through the video and photographic evidence began. Meanwhile, the public was informed by individual agencies and through a series of organized press conferences.

Taken together, that seems like a very good performance. We can all point to elements where it could be further improved. But the standard can't be an unrealistic expectation of perfection. Our question has to be this: Did the response accomplish what could reasonably have been expected, given the intrinsic nature of the event itself—the surprise, the physical and emotional shock, and the inevitable chaos of the immediate aftermath. We believe that the response in Boston was as good as one could reasonably have hoped. This then begs explanation, and forms the basic question of our research: Why were people and organizations able to provide as effective a response as this was? What were the strengths of that response, and what enabled them? And where were the weaknesses—and what can we do to further minimize them? These were the questions at the heart of our research.

I want to emphasize three elements of our research findings about where these features of the response "came from"—that is, what caused or created them:

First, the core underlying reason for the effectiveness of the response in the moment was the rapid formation of an effective command and coordination structure that oversaw and directed all elements of the response. Senior officials from a wide range of agencies—Federal, State, local, and private—felt an immediate need to find one another and join into a concerted and unified command structure and were then able to do so reasonably quickly.

Second, none of that was due to chance—it resulted from literally tens of thousands of hours of joint work, planning, exercises, and operations combining numerous agencies over many years in the planning for and production of fixed events ranging from the Democratic National Convention in 2004 (an event that got particularly attentive focus because it was the first National political convention after 9/11) to the Boston Marathon to the July 4 concert and fireworks on the Esplanade to Patriots and Red Sox and Bruins and Celtics victory parades. Each of those events provided an opportunity—and opportunity that was taken—to practice the process of planning and doing things together. This built knowledge of one another's assumptions and priorities and procedures, fostering understanding and mutual respect of individual and organizational competence and capabilities across agencies. This was the infrastructure that enabled command and coordination to be established quickly and to function effectively after the bombs exploded.

Third, others can do this, too. To be sure, some of the features that contributed to the effectiveness of the response in Boston were unique to Boston. Boston has eight Level I trauma centers, for example, and by happenstance they are arrayed in every direction around the area where the bombs went off, so the injured could be transported in many different directions, reducing congestion among emergency vehicles. Some other elements were unique to the moment—for example, the fact that the marathon takes place on a State holiday, when hospitals are open and fully staffed, but are not doing elective surgery, meant that dozens of operating rooms were immediately available. A shift change was underway at the time of the bombing, which increased availability of skilled hands when they were needed. So there were elements of good fortune that reduced the terrible consequences on that awful day. But most of what made the response as effective as it was can be undertaken by other communities as readily and as well as it was by Boston. Any community can engage in joint planning across its agencies for any major fixed event—from a high school football victory parade to a Fourth of July celebration. Any community can find opportunities to engage in joint planning with other jurisdictions, and with other levels of government—both Federal and State.

On a good day, joint planning and practicing inter-agency coordination—and carrying that out through an incident command structure—is helpful in making events go more smoothly. Paying your dues on the good days by building the infrastructure of interagency familiarity, respect, knowledge, and trust thus has an immediate pay-off—and if a bad day ever comes, that infrastructure is literally a life-saver.

The single most important lesson of our research is that routine and constant practice and use of incident command is one of the best investments a community can make in its present well-being and against any future dark day that might arise.

That said, there are still some things about the command and coordination processes that need some additional work. Our research suggested three areas where further work needs to be done on the development and implementation of incident command:

(1) *Distinguishing between strategy/policy issues and tactical/operational issues.*—In a crisis situation, some of the issues raise policy questions that should be answered by elected political leaders, while other issues are more tactical and operational. Incident management is largely silent on the establishment of processes and procedures for identifying and separating these issues and getting appropriate resolution of them. NIMS focuses almost exclusively on the resolution of tactical issues and on organizing processes for carrying out the indicated operations once the issues have been decided. More attention needs to be devoted in the doctrine to making this distinction, to developing training to help officials practice the distinction, and to building an appropriate structure for interaction between policy makers and operational leaders. This interaction generally worked well in Boston, but not because of the doctrine. In fact, Boston's experience may provide some guidance about what the doctrine should say. For example, the decision to issue a shelter-in-place request was appropriately framed as a policy issue by operational commanders and was put to political leaders for resolution, and this may provide a good illustration of the kind of process of issue identification and resolution that needs to be addressed in the doctrine. It is imperative for NIMS to provide more guidance about the process by which tactical commanders should work in conjunction with an appropriate process for decision making by elected leaders. Both have important but different roles to play, and NIMS currently lacks systematic ways to help these two groups each to stay within their own designated "lane."

(2) *Helping senior operational commanders resist being pulled unduly toward tactical decision making and away from advising political leaders on strategic issues.*—Related to the challenge of distinguishing policy questions from tactical issues, the natural flow of work in incident management structures tends to exert a strong pull on the senior commanders of operational agencies toward being involved in tactical decision making—at precisely the moment when they are also needed to help frame and provide advice to political leaders about more strategic issues. Illustratively, during the Monday afternoon discussions at the unified command at the Westin Copley Hotel, the Governor asked everyone to

put their phones down. The phones represented the pull on the senior operational leaders (by their subordinates) toward engagement with the (many and important!) tactical issues; the Governor wanted their attention to advise him on the (fewer, but even more important!) strategic issues. The attention of senior operational officials is a key resource for both tactical and strategic issues, so we need to develop better doctrine and associated training about how to focus and parse their concentration.

(3) *Developing more effective processes for quickly establishing "micro-command" at the tactical level.*—While coordination, cooperation, and command among the senior leadership of the agencies involved was very strong during the week of April 15 in Boston, better doctrine and training need to be developed to produce similar results when lower-level officials from different agencies encounter one another in the midst of tactical challenges—as occurred in Watertown in the early morning hours of April 19 and then again later that evening. By virtue of doctrine and years of joint planning and practice and work on multi-agency events, the senior leaders of the relevant organizations for the most part knew one another personally and had knowledge of and confidence in each other's capabilities—and they were able rapidly to form unified commands, both on Monday afternoon and again in Watertown in the early hours of Friday morning. Individual police officers arriving from other jurisdictions at the scene of the gunfight at Dexter and Laurel Streets Watertown had none of those advantages to help them form a coordinating structure. We need better doctrine, procedures, training, and practice to aid in the more rapid development of a command structure among people from different agencies arriving more or less independently and not under a pre-existing overarching command structure. We refer to this as the problem of establishing "micro-command," and dealing with this requires that the doctrine that is now working well to coordinate agencies at the senior level needs to be cascaded downward so that it functions at any level where the agencies may encounter one another.

The problem of micro-command needs a bit of further explanation. The issue is illustrated by the difference between what happened within the Watertown Police Department (including both officers and dispatchers), on the one hand, and what happened with arriving officers from other jurisdictions, on the other, at the scene of the gunfight at Dexter and Laurel streets. Watertown officers were first on the scene; they knew each other, knew their command structure, were in direct radio contact with one another, recognized each other's voices, and had good situational awareness about where they were, where their assailants were, and what the street map around them looked like. As a result, they were able to coordinate their actions against their assailants and moved against them in a way that, considering the circumstances—they were being fired upon and having explosive devices thrown at them—seems to have been both coherent and largely effective. Their assailants arrived in Watertown armed with a semi-automatic handgun and enough ammunition to reload it at least once and with a collection of explosive devices; at the end of the confrontation with Watertown police, one was dead and though the other temporarily escaped and may still have been dangerous, he was no longer armed when he fled the scene. As a result of the "micro-command" structure they automatically brought with them to the scene by virtue of being from the same department, the Watertown Police Department officers engaged their assailants in an organized and effective way and coordinated well with the WPD dispatch team.

Arriving officers from other jurisdictions, by contrast, did not know one another, did not know the surrounding area, did not have their own command structure present to help organize or guide them, and did not find nor did they immediately form a command structure that could help deploy them effectively. They were, in effect, forced to act on more or less uncoordinated individual initiative. To some extent, this is inevitable in the early moments of an intense and confusing engagement when people from different jurisdictions show up to help. And, to the credit of those present, micro-command was eventually established at the various sites in Watertown where significant police actions took place (of which there were several). In general, however, it required the arrival of very senior officers before the others present were able to recognize and to accept command. Some of these events involved crossfire situations that endangered fellow officers and nearby residents, so the need to develop an approach that will minimize such circumstances in the future is urgent.

Let me now turn to my second message today, about the community part of resistance to terrorism that was on display last year in Boston and is on display this year as my daughter and Chief Deveau and thousands of others train to run in this year's marathon—and yet more thousands of others prepare to make the event both smooth and safe. It is about the community's part in "Boston Strong"—the local description that encompasses what everyone from first responders to bystanders to community members did to stand tall and proud in the face of two murderous thugs with terrorist intent.

Boston Strong is not a form of hubris or arrogance or naïveté—but a form of pride and defiance and resilience.

Terrorists are, in the end, few and weak—which is, of course, why they choose the methods they use. We are many, and large, and strong. We could never be defeated by them—but we could voluntarily surrender to them . . . and we must not. If we cower in fear, if we abandon our commitment to a free and open society, then we do their work for them. We cannot defend the American way of life—which, importantly, includes our liberties—by surrendering that way of life.

In every generation since our predecessors stood on the Lexington Green and at Old North Bridge in my hometown of Concord, Massachusetts—indeed, since their predecessors came ashore at Jamestown and at Plymouth—men and women have fought and some have bled and some have died to defend the American way of life. In the last century and a half—until 9/11—nearly all of that took place on foreign soil, and the Americans defending our way of life were mostly men and women in uniform. In an age where terrorism is an occasional fact of modern life, some of the battlefields are, unfortunately, now in the homeland and so the "soldiers" in that conflict now sometimes include ordinary Americans going about their daily lives. Resilience—psychological resilience by ordinary Americans in the face of the threat, and even in the face of casualties—therefore has to be seen as a core part of our defense strategy against terrorism.

Preserve, protect, uphold, and defend—Boston Strong affirms the oath of office. Boston Strong says that we will defend the American way of life by continuing to participate in it.

The community part of Boston Strong is a pretty good place to start in thinking about what resilience looks like—and perhaps about how to build it.

Our full report contains more detail about the events and further discussion of the key implications and lessons about the challenges of organizing and operating command and coordination in events like this. For purposes of my testimony here, let me now enumerate more completely the main recommendations from our research:

STRATEGIC COMMAND

- *Senior leaders should participate in a unified command at the strategic level and avoid being pulled back into making tactical decisions and directly overseeing basic operations.*—While some engagement with rapidly evolving tactical matters is necessary, top commanders should concentrate on working with their peers in other organizations to establish an integrated, cross-agency, policy perspective that looks at the big picture context and a longer time frame.
- *The management of intra-organizational, tactical matters should be undertaken by the next tier of institutional leaders,* who should be carefully prepared in advance through training, exercises, and actual experience to assume these responsibilities during crises.
- *To help ensure leaders' strategic focus and opportunity for effective coordination with peers, contingency plans for fixed events like the marathon should provide for well-equipped, secure facilities for top commanders to work together in the event of an emergency.*—This command post should be close to but separate from the location of subordinates who manage tactical operations.
- *Organizations must develop sufficient depth of leadership so that they can rotate personnel regularly during extended events; otherwise, they will inevitably falter from fatigue.*—By Friday evening, many of the people managing the overall event had been awake for 36 or more hours and, more generally, had been sleep-deprived since Monday's bombing. Both they and their deputies had been more than fully deployed throughout the event, leaving no unused (rested) capacity in the system. Failure to provide for sufficient downtime for senior officials inevitably degrades their judgment, ability to comprehend information, and performance of even normal tasks. Allowing for regular rotation requires creating more personnel depth in these leadership positions.
- *Senior leaders should not to be unduly exposed to the enormous flow of raw information, lest their attention be diverted from strategic issues and problems.*—In an event with 24/7 news and social media saturation, there is an enormous amount of information circulating at any given time, much of which is misleading or wrong. This stream of data needs to be filtered and organized for top-level leaders so they can concentrate on interpretation and strategic issues.

TACTICAL/LOCAL COMMAND

- *Response organizations must develop procedures and practices to better control "self-deployment" by individual personnel to the scene of emergency action.*— Dangerous situations that threatened both responders and bystanders developed at the scene of the Thursday night shootout and Friday apprehension of the second suspect in Watertown, in part because of an overload of individual public safety officers operating as individuals rather than in disciplined units.
- *Public safety organizations should develop improved doctrine, better training, and practice through exercises to ensure effective "micro-command" in crises.*— While officers typically look for command authority when operating at a scene with groups from their own agencies, they are less likely to do so when they have deployed as individuals and arrive at an emergency site on their own. Except for situations when near-instantaneous action is required to preserve life, doctrine should be developed and officers should be trained to look for authority at a scene of mass action, even if command is taken by someone from another organization.
- *Improved discipline and training is needed to control weapons fire when public safety officers from many organizations are present.*—Control over fields of fire and authorization to fire is another critical micro-command issue in any rapidly-evolving, high-stress, emotion-laden event. It is dramatically more complicated when a "sudden team" of people from different agencies are thrown together under circumstances where there is no pre-determined command structure.
- *Improved protocols and control systems for parking emergency vehicles at an actual or potential emergency site must be developed and effectively communicated/emphasized to officers by dispatchers and on-scene commanders during an event to prevent obstruction of further movement that may be required.*
- *In complex, multi-agency events, teams of responders in the field should be structured to take advantage of both the local knowledge of conditions that the "home" organization possesses and the quantity and specialized resources that outside reinforcements can bring.*

PUBLIC COMMUNICATION

- *Maintaining regular and open communication with the public—through traditional and social media—should be a high priority for senior officials, even when confidential investigations are on-going.*—When accurate, frequent, official communications were absent, news and social media filled the gap, sometimes with speculation and misinformation. Development of protocols for crisis communication, incorporating utilization of social media, should be part of the planning for fixed events. This should include improving practices for dispelling widely-disseminated, inaccurate information or rumors.
- *Systems for coordinating and communicating information to families of individuals missing or injured in a crisis need to be improved, perhaps including revision of HIPAA rules governing the release of personal information about patients receiving care during public safety emergencies.*

PREPARATION FOR FUTURE CRISES

- *Robust development, practice, exercise, and application of incident management processes and skills (codified in the NIMS system) greatly enhance the ability of emergency responders to operate in complex, multi-organizational, cross-jurisdictional crises.*—The great value of common systems and the understanding that these produce among responders who have never previously met or worked together should not be under-estimated. They can literally be life-savers for responders and others at a crisis scene.
- *"Fixed" or planned events can be effective platforms for practicing incident management skills even when no emergency occurs, and they are highly useful if emergency contingencies materialize at a fixed event as happened at and after the 2013 Boston Marathon.*—Skills honed at such events can also prepare responders and response organizations to perform more effectively even in "no notice" emergencies that may occur at other times.
- *Because coordinating multiple agencies and disciplines will be particularly difficult in "no notice" events, senior commanders should:*
    - Themselves form a unified command structure to make decisions and implement them,
    - Identify a separate staging area to which deploying individuals and organizations should report and await before undertaking field operations,

- Establish protocols for the formation of "sudden" teams composed of individuals from different organizations that may not have previously worked together.
- *Community resilience should be systematically developed and celebrated.*—In the face of the bombing, Boston showed strength, resilience, even defiance—and these were key drivers of the overall outcomes that is, of "Boston Strong." These qualities are latent in many communities in the United States and elsewhere. Celebrating examples of community resilience—both local examples and from farther afield—may help to cultivate a culture of confidence and self-reliance.

These are the central lessons that we have drawn from this difficult experience—from which we, with others emerge with a combination of sorrow and pride and resolve.

So let me close where I opened: I thank the committee for the opportunity to present the findings of our report, I commend the committee for its historic role in mandating the platform from which the first responder's part of Boston Strong sprang, and I offer the community part of Boston Strong as a positive model of the psychological resilience that is an essential part of the successful defense of the American way of life in a sometimes-threatening modern world.

I look forward to your questions.

Chairman MCCAUL. Thank you, Professor.

Let me just say, we were all—on that day, we were all citizens of Boston that day. The way Boston, the people responded with resilience, with strength, was truly inspiring, I think, to the Nation. I am wearing my "Boston Strong" pin to show my support and solidarity, as well. So thank you for that.

The Chairman now recognizes himself for 5 minutes.

Commissioner Davis, welcome back.

Mr. DAVIS. Thank you.

Chairman MCCAUL. You know, it has been almost a year, as we come up on the anniversary. You know, they say a man's true character is tested in a time of crisis. Sir, your character really shined. You were a true leader. You were a calming influence for the Nation, a comforting influence for the Nation, in a very dangerous time of crisis. I can't think of a better man at a better time than you, sir.

Mr. DAVIS. That is very kind of you. I had a great team, Mr. Chairman.

Chairman MCCAUL. I know I speak for all of us on this committee to say how much respect not only we have but the Nation for your service and your dedication. You will be remembered for a very long time for that.

You and I have talked quite a bit since that tragic day. Your response efforts were heroic and brought an end to these terrorists who were on their way to Times Square.

Can you tell me, in terms of lessons learned—and, again, I don't want this to be a "gotcha" exercise. I never intended it to be that way. But I always think, when something like this happens, we can always analyze and evaluate and determine what, if anything, we can do better to make sure that this never happens again.

Can you tell me, just personally, from your background and experience from this event and your law enforcement background, what are the real lessons learned from the Boston bombing?

Mr. DAVIS. Well, Mr. Chairman, I would like to commend you for the work that you have done, Congressman Keating and all the Members of the committee that have reviewed this. I have taken a good, long look at the report that came out. I think that the recommendations that are broken down into four categories in the report are really the best steps to take to deal with any shortcomings that were identified.

There is nothing in there that can't be accomplished fairly simply. Those recommendations will cause a more comprehensive and effective system to protect our Nation to be put in place, and I think that those should be followed.

Chairman MCCAUL. Right, I appreciate that. I was, as I said in my opening statement, pleased to see that the FBI has begun to implement these recommendations, along with the Department of Homeland Security. That is oversight, I think, at its best. Thank you again for your service, sir.

Chief Deveau, you and I have talked about the tragic events that day but also the acts of heroism on the part of you and your officers, Sergeant Pugliese, in taking down one of the biggest terror threats since 9/11.

What I was interested and maybe surprised to find out was that, once he was taken down, you weren't even quite sure who this person was and then, after the fact, learned that he was indeed the Boston bomber.

Can you tell me—and you and I talked about this. You know, always hindsight is 20/20. But would it make sense to include local police departments in the Boston community or in any community, when something like this happens, when a terrorist attack occurs, after the event occurs, to bring in the local police departments in the area for briefings and for participation with the Joint Terrorism Task Force?

Chief DEVEAU. Thank you, Mr. Chairman.

Yes, I do think so. I believe that—you know, Watertown is a 65-man department. You know, Boston has all the resources; the big cities have that. But Watertown kind of represents most police departments across the country. We have limited resources, and it doesn't make sense for us to have somebody at the JTTF on a full-time basis.

But when something like this happens in my community or in any community across the country, we need to have access to that table and be brought into it, be updated, and play a role there.

I think some of the recommendations that you are making in your report touch on that. We needed to have a seat right away, and there were obstacles that we had to do before we could. So I think there can be improvement. Your committee is helping to make that happen, so I appreciate it.

Chairman MCCAUL. I appreciate your insight on that. I think that that is a potential future recommendation, that local police departments be brought into these crisis situations so you can possibly identify the suspect before rather than after the fact.

But, again, I just want to commend you and Sergeant Pugliese and all the officers, the four behind you, for one of the biggest acts of heroism. You are correct; for 8½ minutes, you were the best police department in the world. I would still argue that you are a great police department. Thanks for your great leadership.

Chief DEVEAU. Thank you, Mr. Chairman.

Chairman MCCAUL. My time has expired.

The Chairman now recognizes the Ranking Member, Ms. Sanchez.

Ms. SANCHEZ. Thank you, Mr. Chairman.

Commissioner Davis and Chief, following the September 11 attacks, the Department of Homeland Security developed the National Incident Management System, NIMS, to improve the ability of first responders to coordinate multijurisdictional response efforts. How have Federal grants enabled response organizations to implement NIMS?

Would reductions to or changes to the structure of our Federal Homeland Security grant programs, such as UASI, et cetera—you know, what the administration is suggesting is we clump everything together in an all-hazards thing and we have at it, versus the different programs that we have set up. Do you feel that the approach by the administration is correct? Would it harm you if we did it that way? Et cetera, et cetera.

Mr. DAVIS. I can tell you from experience that the programs, as they are set up, have been very effective. Our ability to coordinate with other agencies, our ability to train on the NIMS system and to game it out on tabletops and in real-life situations when we were dealing with the sports victories and things like that in Boston, that money all comes from our Homeland Security grants and UASI funding.

The other thing that we have is the equipment that is necessary to respond to something like this. Before the UASI program, our equipment was antiquated and not up to the task. When we were called to service that day, we had exactly what we needed to go in and clear the neighborhoods and do the work that had to be done in Watertown to catch these guys.

So I think the program as it exists works very well.

Ms. SANCHEZ. Chief.

Chief DEVEAU. I would agree with the commissioner's comments. You know, in Watertown, we don't get as much funding as Boston would, nor should we. But Watertown partners with 50 communities that surround Boston, and——

Ms. SANCHEZ. So you are in a UASI together, or——

Chief DEVEAU. Yeah.

Ms. SANCHEZ. Like, in my area, I have two UASI grant recipients, Santa Ana and Anaheim, California, two large cities. But they work through the localized police departments to make sure that everybody is buying things that everybody can interoperably use. You know, I don't need a SWAT thing, but if we need a SWAT situation, you got the right stuff over there.

Is that the way that you do it with your 50 jurisdictions?

Chief DEVEAU. Well, that is exactly right. It makes no sense for Watertown to buy SWAT equipment or a vehicle, but it makes all the sense for Watertown to partner with 50 cities and towns that surround Boston and team up. So, in my department, it doesn't make sense for me to have a SWAT team, but it makes all the sense in the world for us to have a 40-man SWAT team made of all those communities, to have a rapid response team, and to have the armored vehicle and the tactical equipment that we can respond.

So Watertown was able to participate with our Law Enforcement Council, along with Boston and the State Police and the National

Guard, and participate and be able to protect our own community. So those grants went a long way.

The training that goes on, you know, you can never prepare for what happened in Watertown, but training makes police officers professional. Training, training, training—we need to do that to be able to perform when we are challenged like we were in Watertown.

Ms. SANCHEZ. I think my police departments are very concerned about all of this being lumped into one line item and also reduced, by the way. Whenever we consolidate programs into one line item, we generally also reduce at the same time the amounts of money available, so that makes it difficult.

Thank you, gentlemen.

I also have a concern about—the Harvard white paper on Boston Marathon bombings identified communication to the public as an incredibly important issue. Particularly in the light of this 24-hour cycle, everybody is trying to put something up, all the rumors that go, all the things that fly, you know, and then get repeated and repeated, and America gets scared or is incensed or whatever goes on—social media, you know, things that we in the Congress face every day but, for a jurisdiction that all of a sudden has a real crisis on its hands, can be difficult.

Can you tell me, what have you done? What did you learn from that experience? Have you set up different protocols of how you share information, what you say to the community, what you say to the public? How have you dealt with that? What are the lessons that we can learn from that?

Mr. DAVIS. The Boston Police Department had a significant presence on social media prior to the event. I don't think you can have an event and then try to stand up a Twitter or a Facebook account. You really have to understand how that works.

In the years before the April 15 bombing, we used Twitter and Facebook to get information out. We don't even do press releases anymore. We just post it on social media.

Ms. SANCHEZ. Really?

Mr. DAVIS. The press monitors our social media account.

What is good about that is that, not only do we speak one-way, you know, not only can we send information out to the public and to the media, but a dialogue exists on social media. So we are actually able to understand how people are——

Ms. SANCHEZ. Reacting, thinking.

Mr. DAVIS [continuing]. Reacting to what we are saying and whether we are getting the real message across that we wanted to get across.

It is a very, very effective means of getting information out to people quickly and effectively in a crisis. There was no cell phone usage—the cell phones shut down at the marathon because of overuse.

Ms. SANCHEZ. Yes, we saw that on 9/11 also.

Mr. DAVIS. Exactly. So we were able to revert to social media and get messages out to people, for instance, who were trying to find loved ones after the event to tell them where to go and what to do.

It is a very, very effective means of communicating with people and speaking back and forth to them. That dialogue is really critical.

Ms. SANCHEZ. Commissioner, and I also want to hear from the chief if you will indulge me, Mr. Chairman, if the chief will, and then I have just a little follow-up question to what you said.

Chief DEVEAU. I will be brief. I think the Boston Police Department did an incredible job about getting the news out and getting reliable information out. I think that when the media came in, there was so much misinformation and I think people relied on the Boston Police Department to get it straight on those 4 days.

In Watertown, we had to notify our residents at 2 o'clock in the morning to shelter in place, and we had a communication system where we could put that telephone notification out encouraging people to shelter in place, notify their neighbors, and that worked as well.

But Boston really assisted us as the manhunt went on all day long to make sure the residents in greater Boston were getting the right information through the social media.

Ms. SANCHEZ. Just quickly, do you think that other agencies, other police departments, are as advanced as you are, Commissioner, and, for example, not even using the traditional media, but going and putting your press releases out?

Mr. DAVIS. No, there are very few departments that do that. But I think it is becoming more and more of a realization among my colleagues and the major city chiefs that this is something that they should invest time in.

Ms. SANCHEZ. Thank you.

Thank you, Mr. Chairman. Yield back.

Chairman MCCAUL. I want it associate myself with the remarks with respect to the response training. I know that the fall before the bombing that Boston's first responders had an emergency response training exercise that was funded with Homeland Security grant dollars, and I know that made a big difference in saving lives that fateful day.

Mr. DAVIS. There is no question.

Chairman MCCAUL. With that, the Chairman now recognizes the gentleman from New York, Mr. King.

Mr. KING. Thank you, Mr. Chairman. Let me at the outset thank you, and Congressman Keating, for the outstanding work you have done on this report. The time and effort you put into it really represents to me the very best of what a committee should be doing, especially when we have such a topic as this, which can inflame emotions, where there can be distortions. The fact that the two of you worked so well together in bringing out this product I think is really a tribute to the two of you, and I thank you and I am proud to be on the committee with you.

Commissioner Davis and Chief Deveau and Sergeant Pugliese, I want to commend you for your heroic efforts that week. Professor Leonard, I want you to know I bring the best wishes of the FDNY, Chief Pfeiffer in particular, who has worked with you over the years and thanks to you for all the assistance you have given to the FDNY.

Commissioner Davis, when we are talking about what was done that week, first of all, and I am not just here to give tribute to you, I am a friend of yours, I have great admiration for you, but I think the calm and the confidence you projected was absolutely essential. But in addition to that, I thought the fact that within moments of the bombing happening, how you were able to call everything into place, securing the site, getting the ambulances, in other words, everything that had to be done was done. Chief Deveau, your men, the fact is they had no idea this was going to happen and you were within minutes involved in the gun fights for their lives and for the lives of the city of Boston. So that has to be a tribute to the training that went on.

How much effort is put into the training every year? Because obviously you can prepare, but you can't prepare. You have to have as many contingencies as possible and I guess hope for the best and then when it happens, all of that can be put into good use.

So, again, I would just ask the two of you, I guess, how much training goes on? In the course of a year, how much training would you put into trying to provide for contingencies like this?

Chief DEVEAU. We try to train as much as we can all the time. I think some of the best training that my department got with the regional team that I explained about is working with Boston. Whenever those championship parades or the celebrations took place, even going back to the Democratic National Convention that was in Boston a number of years back, we always worked with them. So that is kind of almost if you will training in itself, that we go in there and help them. So we support them.

But we train all the time. Our units train kind-of with Boston, with the State police, trying to do that. I think, you know, it kind-of looks like a sports team. A sports team practices, practices, practices to get it right on game day, and that is what we need to do. We need to train, train, train to make sure we are able to do that. Dollars are limited, it is hard to do, but I think we try to put it in the right ways, the money that we do get Federally. With Ed Davis' leadership I think we have done a great job in the greater Boston area in working together and having that work, and that unified command of everybody doing it that particular day was based on all the training that we have done with the cities and towns around Boston with Boston.

Mr. DAVIS. So there was a very specific training that occurred in the year prior to the marathon where we put a Mumbai-style attack scenario together and we used UASI to fund a full day—actually it was a couple of days of training. We took over several different venues in the city and played out what would happen if there were multiple attacks on the city.

That was the first time we had engaged the medical people into the training. So that was called Operation Urban Shield. It was very effective because it got the medical people lined up with us. When we went to the hospitals and had to take over some of the emergency rooms because there were potential suspects there, I think because we had done training with them before-hand, it went much more smoothly. That same year we had done a Homeland Security training that came in through DHS, so two huge trainings in addition to a continual process of training for our SWAT teams that happens routinely.

Mr. KING. Commissioner, if I could ask you, we have already gone over the issue of the information not being shared before the event and that has been discussed and is apparently is being addressed, but also coming from New York I was struck by the fact that Dzhokhar, when he was being interrogated in the hospital, that is when it came out about Times Square. But the NYPD and nobody in New York was told about that by the FBI.

Now, at that time, no one knew that those two brothers were the only two involved. It could have been a conspiracy and there could have been others on their way to New York, and yet New York was not told about it, and Commissioner Kelly first learned about it 2 or 3 days later and he called me up on the phone asking why I didn't tell him. I told him I didn't know anything about it. I don't think anyone knew about it other than the FBI in Boston.

Going toward the future, what is the protocol if you do find a possible, additional attack that is being planned? Should that police department be notified? It could have been Philadelphia, it could have been anyone along the Atlantic coast there.

Mr. DAVIS. I really think that we may be holding this information too closely in the interests of prosecution or having justice be the only thing that we think about, because in addition to justice, there is the issue of public safety and allowing people to get systems in place if there is a wider conspiracy.

So I really—you know, our system is so focused on close hold and maintaining all the evidence for the prosecution. That is certainly, you know, the right thing to do, but I think that singular focus must be tempered with the overall safety and security of the community.

Mr. KING. Because for all we knew at that moment there could have been another attack being planned in another city, New York, Philadelphia, Trenton, whatever.

Mr. DAVIS. I understand Commissioner Kelly's concern.

Mr. KING. Thank you, commissioner and chief. Let me say about Chief Deveau, like others on the committee, I was up in Watertown to find out exactly what happened and not only did he give me a minute-by-minute briefing, but he stood in the pouring rain for an hour which was above and beyond the call of duty. Maybe you can get a line-of-duty disability for that.

Thank you for coming. I thank all the witnesses. Yield back.

Chairman MCCAUL. I thank the gentleman.

The Chairman recognizes the gentleman from Massachusetts, Mr. Keating.

Mr. KEATING. Thank you, Mr. Chairman. I would like to ask unanimous consent to clarify for the record in Congressman Sanchez's statements that it was Dzhokhar Tsarnaev that is the bomber in Federal custody.

Chairman MCCAUL. Without objection, so ordered.

Mr. KEATING. Thank you, Mr. Chairman.

Like so many other people, I wondered what the motivations behind the attack were, how it came to be and how it could be prevented in the future. Because of that, it took me to Russia two times to try and get some information to see if there was a link between the North Caucasus region, Dagestan and Chechnya, and if there was any connection for the motivations of this. In the course of doing that, I learned that authorities here in the United States, the FBI and later the CIA, were given detailed information about Tamerlan Tsarnaev through Russian security services and pursuing this information back home I did encounter some frustration with our own Federal agencies in that regard.

There is a real concern about information sharing across the board, but there is an obvious multiplier benefit in sharing information. In the testimony before this committee this year, we were told that there is roughly 800,000 local police that could be utilized in this effort, and there is about 14,000 FBI agents. One of the sensitivities behind the lack of information sharing, at least I found as a DA, is a concern that as you spread information even among law enforcement sources, there could be leaks, and there is that inhibition.

I would like to ask all of you, to me in your jobs right now people's lives are in danger and you already hold very sensitive information that if that information were released in your own communities, that people could be in danger. So could you comment on how you have maintained that confidentiality every day, and how I think there is a greater risk in not sharing that information with local police authority?

Mr. DAVIS. Well, since 9/11, police chiefs around the Nation have received Secret and Top Secret clearances so that they can be involved in the conversation around these issues, and the intent of that was to make sure that there was wider distribution, wider spreading of the type of information that would be helpful to Ed in Watertown and to myself when I was in Boston. So I think that the intent is really good and I think that people have recognized that that should be the way it works.

But when you are dealing with such large organizations over a period of time, sustaining change is difficult. That elastic band tends to pop back to where it was. So besides having good intentions and having good policies, there has to be a constant testing of systems to make sure that they are, in fact, working, and I think that is where we need some work.

Mr. KEATING. Chief, did you have a comment?

Chief DEVEAU. Yes, I would agree. I think depending on what the intelligence is, it needs to get down to our level. It is our officers that are on the street that are interacting, and it is a value added. There could be more information that they are not aware of that the officers behind me are aware of and we can share information. I think we have to continue to build that trust and move forward and use this as an example to get better.

Mr. KEATING. I had another question. During the whole course of this, this committee has tried to really have a continuum of what happened before with initial information, what happened during the attack, what happened afterwards, and I think this committee has done very well to fill in all those areas. There is an area that I still have questions about, and I want to learn about this, particularly former Commissioner Davis could be helpful in this regard, because there is an area, and I want to see procedurally what was going on, and I think we could do that without jeopardizing anything frankly at all.

There was a *60 Minutes* segment just recently that was broadcast nationally about the marathon bombing and the FBI's response that put into play for that and I learned for the first time in that segment that the images that ended up being the images of the suspects, those images were available on Wednesday. Furthermore, I recall on Wednesday there was a press conference that was announced for National audience, I believe at the Boston police station or wherever it was being held and then at the last minute, that was canceled.

Now, could you shed light on what was the nature of that press conference being called, and why it was canceled and if there is some procedure in that period that took place or some steps to fill in that blank period I have?

Mr. DAVIS. We did have the photographs on Wednesday and there was a press conference scheduled, but at that point in time, the FBI had taken jurisdiction of the case so they were making the decisions on when the press conferences would be or not. It was a desire among everyone at the table to be out front on this as often as possible, but at that particular juncture, I think there was a decision made somewhere above me that there would not be a press conference. But that was between the FBI and the Justice Department people.

Mr. KEATING. You don't know the reason behind that?

Mr. DAVIS. I have no idea.

Mr. KEATING. Or what happened in that 24-hour stretch before that there was another press conference?

Mr. DAVIS. Right.

Mr. KEATING. To me, and thank you for being that candid, to me that just goes to show one more time that maybe there should be more information sharing at all times during this too, because I would have thought whatever that period, whatever was going on during that period, frankly the Boston police should have known what was going on.

I will just yield back my time, Mr. Chairman. I appreciate that.

Chairman MCCAUL. Thank you, Mr. Keating.

The Chairman recognizes Mr. King for the purposes of entering a question into the record.

Mr. KING. Professor Leonard, the FDNY through Chief Pfeiffer has just asked me if I would ask this question, if you could submit the answer in writing. It is important to them. They have worked on it with you.

You mentioned the idea of micro-command as an issue that needs to be better addressed in the NIMS system. What exactly did you mean by that and why is it important? If you could submit a written answer to that I would be very appreciative. Thank you.

Thank you, Mr. Chairman.

Chairman MCCAUL. The Chairman recognizes the gentleman from Pennsylvania, Mr. Meehan.

Mr. MEEHAN. I thank you, Mr. Chairman, and I thank each and every one of your distinguished guests for being here today. Let me just say one thing, in addition to the way you responded in the past with all of your officers, I know, Sergeant, you were talking about, and Chief Deveau, you are going to run in this next marathon, and the idea that it is not just how we responded in the past but the resolve to demonstrate to those who want to create terror in our communities that it is not going to happen, and the idea that the nurses and the officers and others are going to run 22 miles in a marathon is a commitment in addition. So thank you for doing that.

Also I want to touch on this thing that Peter mentioned because I think, and I appreciate the professor's focus on this, the concept of incident command was really a significant achievement. I know it is something that is practiced, but as a former prosecutor, I appreciate that while you were responding, Chief Davis, you were doing two things. The first and foremost you were responding to make sure that people who were injured were safely evacuated, and it was remarkable that within a half an hour, those people whose lives could have been lost were in trauma centers being taken care of. But at the same time, you were securing an incredible crime scene. That is the very substance of the information that becomes subsequently the evidence with chain of custody and other kinds of things that are necessary for the prosecution we are trying to protect. So I appreciate the concept of chain of command.

But there really are two questions, and Peter asked one of them, and I would be interested in having the two chiefs and professor, if you have a moment. When you were making decisions and in that chain of command, and there were a couple of different kinds of things. There was a distinction between policy decisions and procedural decisions. That is where you get the command structure which includes those of you who know the policy or the procedures about how to secure a crime scene, how to keep a community safe, how to respond and put your officers in.

But there is also questions. You made a determination to release the photographs of the two individuals. You made a determination to shut the city down for a period of time, to secure Watertown, a remarkably courageous political decision.

If you can discuss how you distinguished between the two and how you worked with sometimes political officials that may not have the same sort of background. Then you were talking about, and, Professor, you focused on this micro, and that was these officers who were responding to the scene. They come, and the unit in Watertown knows each other, but in small communities, you know, it could be the next town over, Reading or Everett or somebody, the officers are coming in and they don't work with these guys. So how do you create a structure where people are rushing in to a scene and the concept of being able to create an effective response? I think we have got after-action assessments of those kind of things and they are all good lessons learned.

So if you can talk about that policy piece, chiefs, and, professor, if you want to take a moment to talk about the issue of the micro, I think it would be helpful for all of us.

Mr. DAVIS. The procedural piece, and these are very astute observations, Congressman, and I appreciate you asking these questions, the procedural piece was fairly much laid out for us through our practicing and through our dealing with homicides, some multiple homicides, that occur in the city day in and day out. So we are frequently called to the scene where people have been badly injured, multiple people have been shot. Our first responsibility is to save lives and get them out as quickly as possible and get them the medical attention that they need.

But very quickly after that, and it happens very fluidly, the crime scene gets locked down. This particular crime scene was complex because there was a distinct possibility that there was a third device there. So we were not only locking the crime scene down to preserve evidence, but to preserve the lives of the first responders. We had everybody leave the scene, leave the field after we got a perimeter set up until the bomb squad could go in and do their work. But it becomes very methodical at that point in time.

So in the 18 minutes it took us to clear the victims, very quickly after that, a process was put in place, EOD clearing and then evidence collection, and one of the first things we did was tell our technical people to start to collect videotape. That videotape played an important role down the road.

But as for the policy decisions, Mayor Menino left the hospital and came to the scene at the command post. He was joined there by Governor Patrick. So our job as police officials, myself, the Colonel from the State police, Rick Deslauriers from the FBI, was to give the political officials enough information so that they could get information out to the public and calm fears, but also make decisions around big political issues like the closing down of the transit system.

Our role was to be advisors. We advised. We told our elected officials exactly what we had. At the time that the decision was made to shut down the transit, there were a series of events that were playing out that gave people the idea that there could very well be a broader conspiracy with other people involved.

So there were courageous decisions made, but it was based on the best information that we had. We provided that to the elected officials and they did their job.

Mr. MEEHAN. Professor, my time is up, but maybe you can jump into that because you have an appreciation for both that aspect, the policy decisions, as well as the micro piece.

Mr. LEONARD. Congressman, like Commissioner Davis, I think you are focused on the most important question here. My message is, don't take incident management for granted. It is not an accident. It takes a lot of work to build and it is incredibly important.

What is important about it is that it facilitates the command and coordination across multiple agencies. Inevitably, the capabilities we need for these big horrible messy events are going to be in multiple different agencies, and they should be. The challenge is how to bring those collectively and creatively together effectively in the moment and that is harder than it looks. It is not self-executing, and it is not a natural act for those agencies to do it. So it has to be practiced in advance.

It has to be worked on and developed. You pointed out all three levels. So there is the political interface with the strategic operational. So the Governor and the Mayor interacting with Commissioner Davis, with Chief Deveau and other operational officials to figure out are we going to shut down the city? Are we going to— the release of the photographs is really a more tactical kind of issue. But that political issue is enormously important, and the National Incident Management System is silent on this question of how that is supposed to work. So that is an area where we need further work. That is the macro level of command and coordination.

The micro level is what Sergeant Pugliese brought to the scene because he is naturally part of a system in which there is command, in which the officers know each other. That is in contrast to the dozens of other officers who showed up from many different departments at the same moment or a little bit thereafter, mostly after the gunfight was over at Dexter and Laurel. They didn't have a natural tactical command structure, and we need to work on that. That is what I mean by micro command.

So we need to work on the continuing coordination and command at all different levels, remembering this is the most important asset, and it is not a natural thing to have happen by itself, and it requires enormous amounts of work and development and practice ahead of time. We can do this.

But I think for me, the most important lesson of this whole experience is that any community can do this, but not every community has done this, and we need to keep at that. Because Boston is strong and the incident management on display in Boston shows what can be done, but we shouldn't assume that it is now universal. We need to keep working on that.

So thank you for asking the question. It is an excellent question.

Mr. MEEHAN. Well, before I yield back, I want to say it is frustrating as a Philadelphia fan to have to realize that you get all this practice because you have all these victory parades with Patriots and everybody else.

Mr. LEONARD. Win the Series and you can practice too.

Chairman MCCAUL. The Chairman now recognizes Mr. Payne.

Mr. PAYNE. Thank you, Mr. Chairman.

Commissioner Davis and Chief Deveau, the administration is proposing to consolidate the Homeland Security programs including UASI and the State Homeland Security Grant Program into one pool. Based on the testimony heard here and some of the comments in Ranking Member Thompson's statement, quite a few of us are concerned about that prospect. Under the proposal, grantees would no longer be required to dedicate 25 percent of their grant awards to law enforcement and terrorism prevention.

Do you have concerns about the proposed consolidation in reference to those grants?

Mr. DAVIS. Congressman, I do. I think that the program as it is set up is working very well. I am not briefed in on the exact idea on the change, but if it results in a reduction in overall money, I think it is problematic.

Mr. PAYNE. Right. As Congresswoman Sanchez stated, sometimes in those consolidations, the amount of the dollars are drawn down as well, consolidated. So that is a grave concern to quite a few of us on this committee and throughout the Congress because we know how those UASI and those grant programs have been exceptional, especially in an area such as mine. I am from North New Jersey and I have the Port Authority, I have the port, the rail, the airport, so the UASI grant has been phenomenal for us in that area.

Chief Deveau, would you like to make a statement in reference to that? Because it says it would no longer require them to dedicate 25 percent of those grants to law enforcement and terrorism prevention activities, and that is what our concern is, that money could be deviated for reasons other than those?

Chief DEVEAU. Congressman, I agree with the Commissioner. I think the current system is working and I think Boston is an example of it working very well. I think it should stay in place.

Mr. PAYNE. Okay. I will yield back in the interest of time.

Chairman MCCAUL. Thank you. We certainly appreciate that. Thank you, Mr. Payne. The Chairman now recognizes Mr. Swalwell from California.

Mr. SWALWELL. Thank you, Chairman, and thank you to our witnesses for being here today. I also as my colleagues have noted stand with Boston and commend you for your work.

Commissioner, you and I spoke before at this hearing and I pointed out that it was Urban Shield Training that your force had gone through, first in Alameda County, which I have the privilege of representing, but also an exercise that you held yourself.

I wanted to bring to the witnesses' and the committee's attention that a year later, we still, I believe, face threats from terrorists, whether abroad or individuals in the United States, rogue actors who may be influenced by publications on the web or that they receive and are able to use materials that are readily available at different stores.

I was disturbed to read and learn in the most recent edition of al-Qaeda's Arabian Peninsula publication *Inspire* there is a picture of a young person sitting in a tram, which is used at San Francisco's international airport, and the English translation with this person sitting in the tram says, "For how long will you live in tension. Instead of just sitting, having no solution, simply stand up, pack your tools of destruction, assemble your bomb ready for detonation."

This is one of the largest international airports in the world, certainly one of the largest on the West Coast, and thousands of passengers a day use the tram to connect from our BART system to the airport. I was wondering if that publication, in its most recent magazine, brings concern to you, Commissioner, about threats still existing.

Mr. DAVIS. Congressman, it is good to see you again and it does bring concern to me. In the month after the April 15 bombing *Inspire* magazine had a whole issue devoted to the Tsarnaev brothers.

This kind of extremist propaganda on the internet, if it is not countered with something, does tend to create problems for us. So we actually are talking about this at the Kennedy School right now trying to get college students engaged in putting proper information out on the web to really fly in the face of what these extremists are putting out there as the truth.

But it goes beyond that. When you see that type of a picture in there, when you read about the attacks on the infrastructure around the transformers in California that were sniped at, it is hard to figure what is real and what isn't real in this area. We need to be vigilant. It is clear that there is a threat and we need to really be aware of it and do everything we can as a Nation to stop it from happening.

Mr. SWALWELL. Commissioner, knowing that, at least in this most recent publication that the San Francisco area is depicted in this al-Qaeda publication, what do you think that would mean for local law enforcement and Federal law enforcement and what do you think they would need to do to coordinate efforts with the resources we provided or resources that you think may, in the future, need to provided?

Mr. DAVIS. Well, the great thing about our country, Congressman, is that each of the police departments has that responsibility and I am sure the officials in San Francisco are looking very closely at this threat. But you just need to be vigilant. That is clearly what needs to happen. I am sure there are a series of inquiries that are occurring around this and what can be done to tighten up the system. That would just make a lot of sense.

Mr. SWALWELL. Just to follow up on Mr. Payne's, my colleague from New Jersey's questioning, is it your position, Commissioner, that you would prefer a grant system through Homeland Security that is not consolidated, as is being proposed? Because as you know, Urban Shield and other exercises are funded through UASI, a specific grant, and that could be threatened should consolidation take place.

Mr. DAVIS. Well, make no mistake, the UASI program works because it goes right to the cities, and the problem is it gets watered down when it gets diverted to the State. So, yes, I think that that is my concern.

Mr. SWALWELL. Thank you, Commissioner.

I yield back the balance of my time.

Chairman MCCAUL. The Chairman recognizes Ms. Clarke from New York.

Ms. CLARKE. Thank you very much, Mr. Chairman, and I thank our witnesses for bringing their experience to bear as we sort of reflect on the response in light of the Boston bombings.

I was a New Yorker, I am a New Yorker and was a member of the New York City Council during the 9/11 event and had jurisdiction in the Council over the rebuilding of the FDNY. So my question really goes to how well we have institutionalized NIMS and my first question goes to Professor Leonard.

In your report you mentioned the response agencies should develop procedures and practices to better control self-deployment, and that is something that we New Yorkers were keenly aware of in the 9/11 event. Can you provide some best practices for the types of procedures and how do you suppose that self-deployment tactics may be warranted in certain situations to prevent immediately threats of death and destruction. How do we strike that balance? Is there a necessity to sort of create some space in the NIMS protocol to address that?

Mr. LEONARD. Thank you, Congresswoman, I think that question goes exactly to the issue that we were trying to raise in the report.

Self-deployment did happen in Watertown. There was also a lot of dispatched—many officers from many other areas were told that they should go. But when they got there, that didn't mean that they had any natural command structure to join in Watertown. So the Watertown Police Department is very organized in its response.

I think to some extent, self-deployment is inevitable in some of these circumstances, and it is also not necessarily a bad thing. So it is not that we are trying to prevent that. The question is: In the presence of self-deployment, when have you a bunch of people from different agencies all arriving in a confused situation, arriving in sequence, because they don't all get there at the same moment, what should they do? We don't have a very good doctrine about that.

We have lots of doctrine about how you can organize at the senior level, and the senior officials who arrived did that. They arrived in Watertown in the middle of night. Chief Deveau found Commissioner Davis and several others and they immediately began to form a command structure at the Watertown Mall.

At the senior level that is all working. It is at the tactical level that we don't really have a doctrine, we don't have training. We can't expect those officers to have known each other before, but we might be able to develop some protocols for how they could combine so that we get something a little bit more organized. The referenced standard for this is not that they should be able to be like a college drill team in a half-time show, but maybe we could provide some doctrine so they could, through training and knowing how to use those protocols, they could establish a somewhat more organized response somewhat more quickly.

In Watertown, senior police officials on some of those incidence scenes were able to eventually get things organized, but it took a little longer than we might like and I think we could develop protocols that would help people to do that faster.

Ms. CLARKE. Chief Deveau, from your experience, what would you take from your experience as to how we can best manage just the inclination of law enforcement and our first responders to create—you know, there is an inclination. People are just going to come knowing what it means to their jurisdiction, their town, their people, their families. What would you say would be something that we could move closer to creating to manage a circumstance like that?

Chief DEVEAU. Thank you, Congresswoman. I think, first of all, that you mentioned NIMS and I think NIMS has worked. I mean, the unified command that we had in Watertown worked very well. So, as has been pointed out, at the command level, it worked because we have all been together. Ed Davis and I have known each other for about 15 years. So when he came walking down that back street in Watertown in the middle of the night we ended up being shoulder-to-shoulder for the next 18 hours and there was complete trust between us. As the other police commissioners showed up, Colonel Alben from the State police and everybody like that.

I think there is a little bit of a disconnect when you get down to another level, when other departments start to show up from various cities and towns. We don't train currently for them to start working together. I think we have to go back and look at that in our academies that when there is somebody of leadership, there is a sergeant or lieutenant on the street, regardless of what town or city he is from, he or she, if they are the highest-ranking person in that area, then they have to have the knowledge and the ability to take control.

We really don't do that well now, and I think it is one of the lessons or takeaways that I see in a lot of people that came to Watertown that we need to do a better job in self-deployment. We needed those officers, but we needed to work a little bit quicker together and better together.

Ms. CLARKE. Mr. Davis, did you want to add anything to that?

Mr. DAVIS. Just briefly, Congresswoman. I think that Ed is correct that at the micro level, Dutch's observations are exactly right. More work needs to be done there. We changed our doctrine after Columbine. Our protocols before Columbine were to secure the area and wait for the SWAT team to arrive. Columbine taught us that we don't have that luxury anymore. So our officers are now trained to put together a contact team and to go in and address the threat.

What we haven't done is come to the realization that that contact team may comprise officers from several different agencies simply because when the call goes out, everybody responds. So how that team is structured and who is in charge of that team, that is sort of the nuts and bolts of this, I think.

Ms. CLARKE. I thank you gentlemen and yield back, Mr. Chairman.

Chairman MCCAUL. Thank you.

The Chairman recognizes Mr. Duncan.

Mr. DUNCAN. I thank the Chairman for the committee hearing, for the report and the excellent work the committee did on that. I will say that I appreciate you bringing up a little moment of silence for the Fort Hood shooting, and South Carolina stands with Texas, just as we stood with Boston last year.

I will say for the record that the Red Sox are my AL team. I am a Braves and Nats fan, but as Mr. Keating and I talk about from time to time, I do like the Sox,

One thing, after reading the report, Mr. Chairman, it kept coming back to me the term "stovepiping" and the failure of sharing information across so many lines that came out after 9/11 and how glaring that is today. The report points out that the information was there if the dots were connected, if the information was shared. I remember the testimony from Commissioner Davis last year about if the JTTF, your officers had been informed and would have had the ability to do a little more research, maybe this tragedy would have been prevented.

So we hear a lot in this committee about lessons learned. Well, doggone it, I am tired of just learning the lessons. We have got to start applying those lessons. I mean, if we will do away with the stovepiping, as a government, as agencies like the FBI or components of DHS are willing to admit that they are not a fiefdom and they can't just control that information and they need to realize they can't be everywhere, nor do we want law enforcement to be everywhere, but if they will rely on the Boston police, the Watertown police, the elements in my State, whether it is the county sheriffs or local city police or whether it is the State law enforcement division, if that information can be more readily shared, I believe we could avert more tragedies.

So, Mr. Chairman, I don't want to sit here a year from now or 2 years from now and have this same conversation about we had all the information, we failed to connect the dots and we failed to let the folks that are closer to the situation let them know about the potential threats, because Government is large and Government is cumbersome in its response to a lot of things. Where the flexibility and true ability lies is on the ground with the guys that can actually ask the questions of the people in the local supermarkets or the churches or the community clubs or the neighborhoods. So I will get off that rant.

But I will say although there unquestionably has been significant progress in 13 years since 9/11 on the issues of the barriers, the walls, the stovepiping and the things that are inhibiting information sharing, full partnership is necessary.

So Commissioner Davis, I know you are not in your role as you were this time last year, but from your perspective could you share with the committee why you believe these barriers remain or if they do remain? Or maybe I am off base on that. I would love to hear your perspective.

Mr. DAVIS. I think we have come a long way. I think Director Comey has done a tremendous job. He said all the right things and done all right things since he has become the new director to address these issues. I had a conversation with Chairman McCaul last night. It appears as though we are moving in the right direction.

But the recommendations that this committee has come up with are exactly the way we should be going to make this a more comprehensive system. But if those recommendations aren't put into a Federal code somewhere, they are simply that, recommendations. So if the Congress in its wisdom sees these things as good things, then it should be codified so that the system has to operate that way. Police agencies at every level follow the law, and if that is the law, that is what they will do. So that rubber band snapping back that we talked about a little earlier, it makes it impossible to do that.

The other thing I want to mention is this is a story of numbers. If there are less than 20,000 Federal agents, FBI agents, working on the issue of terrorism, and there are 600,000 local police officers, we are a force multiplier. That has to be a recognition on the part of all agencies that if we are going to have a comprehensive—I have had the ability to work in the United Kingdom and other police agencies in other countries where there is a system from top to bottom, and that really should be our model so that everybody is working together and everybody recognizes this isn't my ball, it basically is everybody's responsibility.

Mr. DUNCAN. Let me just ask you, wasn't that the original purpose of the JTTF?

Mr. DAVIS. Yes. I think the FBI came 90 yards down the field by establishing the JTTFs, but I think that there was some bureaucracy that prevented it to go over the goal line. I think we are right there right now. Those recommendations push it over the goal line.

Mr. DUNCAN. Well, I tell you, I sit in the stands and watch a lot of football games. I am a former football player and enjoy the sport.

I am glad you used that analogy. But one thing that frustrates me sitting in the stands is when I see the coach run the ball up the middle over and over and over and they are getting a yard, a yard-and-a-half, when maybe around the outside or throwing a pass, an end-around or something like that would be more effective. The fans around me are hollering at the coach, why are you running the ball up the middle again?

So sitting in the stands here and looking at the JTTF concept, looking at the failures that are pointed out in this report, I hope the coach, so to speak, reads this. I hope we don't continue running the ball up the middle and getting that yard-and-a-half or getting down to the goal line and not being able to get across. We don't need 99 percent. Those are the lessons learned. One hundred percent gets us across the goal line. We learn from those lessons, we apply those lessons and we keep America safe.

I hope they listen to you. I hope they listen to all you guys that were involved in this. I hope they will read the report, the ones that can make the decisions.

Mr. Chairman, you are doing a great job in pointing this out, laying out the roadmap, and we have, I think, a responsibility and I think we are doing a good job of telling the respective agencies where we need to go, laying out the direction, but not just laying them out, actually cranking the car up and helping them proceed down that road. So I thank you for that.

Thank you guys. God bless you. May God bless Massachusetts, the folks in Boston, all the victims and families, and may God continue to bless America because America was with Boston that day.

With that, I will yield back.

Chairman McCAUL. Let me just close by saying, having worked with the Joint Terrorism Task Force, they do good work. It is a good model. It works 99 percent of the time. We have to be right 100 percent. In this particular case I think there were some things that fell through the cracks. But it is our job not to make people feel bad about that, but see how we can do better in the future so we don't have one of these events again.

These one- to two-man operations are very, very difficult to detect and disrupt. That is the new evolution of both terrorism, of al-Qaeda, radical extremists, and that is what we need to stop.

I do, as Commissioner Ed Davis said, I do want to commend the new FBI director, Comey, for ushering in, I think, a new era at the FBI, a model of cooperation. I have talked to him about the State and local cooperation. I think State and locals are a great force multiplier to an agency that is very resource-strapped. The locals know the streets. They are the eyes and ears on the ground and it makes perfect sense. I think it is indicative that one the first things that Director Comey did was to bring police chiefs to the table to enter into a memorandum of understanding with the police chiefs so that the police chiefs will actually know what their officers are doing on the JTTFs, because that wasn't happening in this case. That needs to change.

I think Director Comey's emphasis of that, I know that his chief of staff is a big State and local fan and I look forward to, I think, a new era which I think will protect Americans ultimately and make America safer.

Commissioner Davis, I think your recommendation to codify these recommendations into law is an excellent idea. Reports come out all the time, recommendations come out all the time, but if it is codified and it has the full force and effect of law, I think that is even stronger. So I commend you for that recommendation as well.

Just to end, I also want to thank the staff on both sides of the aisle for all the work they put into this report, particularly Alan Carroll on my staff, who has worked day in and day out for a year with all the relevant agencies doing a great job.

I want to thank Bill Keating, my dear friend from Massachusetts. This hit home to you. But working together with you in developing this report, traveling with you to Moscow to conduct interviews, you and I have been joined at the hip on this report and I think it is very significant.

But our heart does go out to the Boston community. As we approach the anniversary of this bombing, this tragedy, I think it will be a time to remember. It will also be a time to heal. But it will also be a time of pride, for Boston is strong. So let me thank the witnesses——

Mr. KEATING. Mr. Chairman, if I could.

Chairman MCCAUL. Yes, Mr. Keating.

Mr. KEATING. Thank you, Mr. Chairman.

I just want to thank the staff. I want to thank you. You have been to Boston. You traveled every footstep of the way on these scenes. I want to thank you for your personal involvement. Congressman King came down to Watertown. This is very important to our area. It is very important to our country going forward. I want to thank our brave law enforcement officers that are here for the work you have done once again. I will say that moving forward, we have been working in our office on legislation which we will share with everyone that will make sure that, you know, some of the positions change, so you could have someone that is more open to cooperation and then he could be replaced or she could be replaced by someone that doesn't share that same.

So I think going forward it is important to get the laws or the codes changed so that we are not having another report that just sits on the shelf, because we can't afford to have this kind of tragedy, and if we can prevent one of them, all our work will be important.

Again, I turn back and again, thank the Chairman for his personal involvement in this important issue.

Chairman MCCAUL. Let me just close by thanking the officers. You are the true heroes to me and this committee. I also want to thank you for my Watertown police patch and pin. I will wear this very proudly.

With that, this hearing is adjourned.

[Whereupon, at 11:51 p.m., the committee was adjourned.]

APPENDIX

QUESTIONS FROM HON. SUSAN W. BROOKS FOR HERMAN "DUTCH" B. LEONARD

Question 1. Dr. Leonard, you noted in your testimony that, "Others can do this too," referencing the ability to replicate Boston's effective response. In the aftermath of the Boston attacks, I held a hearing in my district to assess Central Indiana's ability to respond to a mass casualty event. I was pleased to hear in this hearing that, like in Boston, there has been extensive pre-event coordination between law enforcement, the fire service, emergency management, and the medical community. How can we most effectively share these best practices to help ensure that other jurisdictions are similarly well-prepared?

Question 2. Dr. Leonard, you mentioned in your written testimony that during a response effort it is imperative that first responders and Government officials maintain regular and open communication with the public and should utilize social media as a platform to reach their communities. I could not agree with you more. My subcommittee held two hearings last year that focused on how social media is transforming the way the Nation responds to and recovers from disasters. A recent survey showed that after a disaster 1 in 5 survivors contact first responders through social media. One of the challenges we discussed during these hearings was the amount of incorrect, misleading, and even malicious information that is posted on social media sites after a disaster. What best practices can we share with other first responders and Government officials to help them validate information posted on social media websites during a disaster?

Answer. Thank you for the privilege of testifying about the findings of our research on the Boston Marathon bombings before your committee. I thought the hearing was well-designed and focused, and I hope it was helpful to you and your colleagues.

I was honored to be a part of it and to appear with some of the true heroes of the hour—the other members of the witness panel, and the Watertown Police Department officers who responded in the early hours of April 19.

In the aftermath of the hearing, you forwarded two written questions to me. I fear that the time for me to respond to them is now past, but hope that these responses may nonetheless still be of some use to you.

The two questions were forwarded from Congresswoman Brooks. She asked, first, about how we can most effectively share the best practices of communities like Boston and her area of Central Indiana that have undertaken the necessary structural pre-work to build an architecture for coordinated response across agencies and jurisdictions under the National Incident Management System.

This is an excellent and important question. As I observed in my testimony, the fact that multiple agencies and jurisdictions could quickly come together and coordinate their actions was crucial to the highly effective performance shown in Boston in the aftermath of the bombing. None of that ability was an accident; it came from years of hard work and practice, as well as from the efforts of DHS, mandated in the basic Homeland Security Act of 2002 (which originated in the House Select Committee that was the predecessor to the committee that you now chair). The best practice, as we outlined it, is for communities to take every available opportunity to practice mutual, coordinated planning and execution—from planning their Fourth of July celebration to handling local football games—by using the National Incident Management System as the basic planning and operational framework for every significant event in their area.

Congresswoman Brooks' question goes to the issue of how we can get other communities to do this—since, as I observed, while every community could do it, not every community has done it. I can't give a fully satisfactory answer—but I would emphasize that one element of our strategy for spreading this practice is bringing greater attention (as we tried to do in our report) to why Boston was able to do as well as it did during that terrible week. These lessons need to be retold and repeated. We are taking every opportunity to speak with public safety officials, political leaders, and community groups about the importance of this kind of practice and of the building in advance of the infrastructure of cooperation. We hope that this finding is something that you and your committee can also help to promulgate.

One device that has been utilized to encourage practicing coordination, and that I think should continue, is providing grants for planning and exercises on a multi-agency, multi-jurisdictional, "regional" basis. The requirement, under DHS grant programs, to undertake joint exercises and to form joint plans has been a useful and effective push in the right direction.

Congresswoman Brooks' second question refers to social media and inquires about the best practices for using and for verifying the information flowing through social media channels during crisis events. Once again, this is a very good question, with no simple answer. One important element is that the effort to utilize social media effectively should not begin at the time of the event; the infrastructure needs to be built well in advance. Public safety organizations need to build a trusted social media voice and populate it regularly during ordinary times, developing a collection of followers who will already be tuned in when a crisis moment breaks. The Boston Police Department had such an effort before the marathon bombing event, and many thousands turned to it in the moment; many say it was the most reliable and accurate source of information about what was known at any given time. This helped to damp down some of the less-grounded posts that were circulating from other sources—and this could only be done during the event because the infrastructure had been built in advance.

As Congresswoman Brooks observes, one of the great challenges of operating in an environment drenched in social media—as crisis events now are—is that many posts from many sources are difficult or impossible to verify. Most putative eyewitness statements are by actual eyewitnesses, and most contain at least some accurate data—but some are complete (and sometimes malicious) fabrications, and even actual eyewitnesses are often confused about what they saw, so even with the best of intentions they may be providing highly misleading characterizations. Even those who are trying their hardest to get and report accurate information are caught in the inevitable fog of war. The simple fact is that there is therefore no straightforward and definitive method for determining which pieces of "information" flowing through social media channels are accurate. In general, the best we can do is to seek confirmation for information that seems important, and to try to differentiate between confirmed/verified claims, on the one hand, and unverified posts, on the other. Again, having a pre-established trusted social media voice for a given agency with loyal followers who have faith in the intentions and competence of the organization is critically important. That voice must then be operated in a way that: (1) Allows it to differentiate as carefully as possible between verified and unverified information, and that (2) keeps pace with the flow of information in the event. If all the official voice can say is that there is no verified information, people will quickly turn to other social media channels. This means that we can neither entirely rely upon, nor entirely ignore, the flow of unverified information in social channels. This is an area where further research and development is needed, but I believe it will remain (and indeed will increasingly become) difficult to manage, and will require operational resources devoted to it in the moment. This may seem like a diversion of resources that are needed elsewhere, but managing perceptions and information during events needs to be seen as a substantive contribution—as much as providing physical assistance.

I hope these observations are helpful to you and the Members of your committee. I would be happy to elaborate further on any of my testimony or any of what I have said here, if that would be of use to you.

Once again, let me thank you for the privilege of appearing before your committee. If there is anything you think I can do that would help advance the important work you are doing, I hope you will not hesitate to let me know.

○